Language Arts Handbook

Level 3

A Division of The McGraw·Hill Companies

Columbus, Ohio

▶ **Consultants:** Jean Wallace Gillet, Charles Temple, and James D. Williams

▶ **Acknowledgments:**

Grateful acknowledgment is given to the following publishers and copyright owners for permissions granted to reprint selections from their publications. All possible care has been taken to trace ownership and secure permission for each selection included. In case of any errors or omissions, the Publisher will be pleased to make suitable acknowledgments in future editions.

From Angel Child, Dragon Child by Michele Maria Surat. © 1983 by Raintree/Steck-Vaughn. All rights reserved. Reproduced by arrangement with Steck-Vaughn Company.

"Kids Did It! In Business" from WORLD Magazine, June 1996. Judith E. Rinard/National Geographic Image collection.

THROUGH GRANDPA'S EYES TEXT COPYRIGHT © 1980 BY PATRICIA MACLACHLAN. Used by permission of HarperCollins Publishers.

"Raccoon" from THE LLAMA WHO HAD NO PAJAMA: 100 FAVORITE POEMS, copyright © 1998 by Mary Ann Hoberman, reprinted by permission of Harcourt, Inc.

"Sardines" from A PIZZA THE SIZE OF THE SUN BY JACK PRELUTSKY. TEXT COPYRIGHT © 1996 BY JACK PRELUTSKY. Used by permission of HarperCollins Publishers.

From THE FASCINATING WORLD OF FROGS AND TOADS by Maria Angels Julivert. English translation copyright © 1993 by Barron's Educational Series. Reprinted by permission.

"A Funny Man" from SING A SONG OF POPCORN by Natalie Joan. Copyright © 1988 by Natalie Joan. Reprinted by permission of rights holder.

"Houses" from UP THE WINDY HILL by Aileen Fisher. Copyright © 1953 by Abelard Press. © renewed 1981 by Aileen Fisher. Reprinted by permission of Marian Reiner for the author.

"The Sun is a Yellow-Tipped Porcupine," from WHIRLWIND IS A GHOST DANCING by Natalia Belting. Copyright © 1974 by Natalia Belting. Used by permission of Dutton Children's Books, an imprint of Penguin Putnam Books for Young Readers, a division of Penguin Putnam Inc.

SARAH, PLAIN AND TALL COPYRIGHT © 1985 BY PATRICIA MACLACHLAN. Used by permission of HarperCollins Publishers.

From THE CITY KID'S FIELD GUIDE. By Ethan Herberman. Copyright © 1989. Reprinted by permission of WGBH Enterprises, Boston, Mass.

From JOHN HENRY by Julius Lester, copyright © 1994 by Julius Lester. Used by permission of Dial Books for Young Readers, an imprint of Penguin Putnam Books for Young Readers, a division of Penguin Putnam, Inc.

www.sra4kids.com

SRA/McGraw-Hill

*A Division of The **McGraw·Hill** Companies*

Send all inquiries to:
SRA/McGraw-Hill
8787 Orion Place
Columbus, Ohio 43240-4027

ISBN 0-07-569539-1

Printed in the United States of America

3 4 5 6 7 8 9   RRC 07 06 05 04 03 02

►Table of Contents

You Are a Writer

Everyone is a writer. You are a writer. Your friend sitting next to you is. Look around you. Everyone you see is a writer.

What Do You Write?

Have you ever made a list of school supplies you needed? Have you ever written a note to your parents? Have you ever written about how to make your favorite food? Maybe you have written a make-believe story. These are a few examples of the kinds of writing you do. Some are long. Some are short. You have probably done many of them already.

When Can You Write?

Anytime! Some people like to write in a journal or a diary before they go to sleep. Others write down words or jokes they might want to use later. Every day, there are many chances to write.

Where Can You Write?

Anywhere! You probably write sitting at a table or desk most of the time, but you can get ideas anywhere. Whether you are outdoors or in your bed, take a second to jot down your ideas.

Why Write?

Everybody has thoughts that are worth sharing. Writing is a way to share your thoughts, ideas, and feelings with others.

How Do You Write?

That question can't be answered in a couple of sentences. That's why there is a lot of help with writing in this book. You will also find information on spelling, punctuation, studying, using the computer, and much more.

New words or phrases are added to the English language as they are needed. For example, *e-mail* and *chat room* are fairly new terms.

The Traits of Writing

Good writers are not born good writers. They learn to be good writers. How? They do it by studying and practicing the traits of good writing. The traits of good writing are certain qualities that make reading it enjoyable. These traits are described below and on the following pages.

Ideas

Your ideas should be clear, original, and supported by details. Ideas are the heart of your writing. Good ideas are supported by colorful details that make writing interesting to a reader. Your writing should have a main idea that sends a clear message to the reader. Use accurate details to support your idea.

Take a Look

Read this paragraph from *Angel Child, Dragon Child* by Michele Marie Surat.

> My sisters skipped through the stone gate two by two. Mother was not there to skip with me. Mother was far away in Vietnam. She could not say, "Ut, my little one, be an Angel Child. Be happy in your new American school."

When you read the paragraph, did you think, "I want to know more about Ut. I like reading about people from other countries"? The author gives enough details to make the reader curious about Ut's culture and care about what happens to her.

Organization

Your writing should have
▶ a beginning that interests the reader right away
▶ a sequence that makes sense
▶ a good ending

A reader who is not interested in your beginning probably will not keep reading for very long. That is why your first few sentences or paragraphs should convince the reader that he or she should read on to the end.

The sequence of events or information should make sense to the reader. If you tell about something that happened in the past, make sure the reader can easily tell that it happened in the past.

Your ending should leave the reader thinking, "That was really good. I will tell my friends to read this."

Take a Look

Read the ending of *Angel Child, Dragon Child.*

> On the last day of school, when I knew the *hoa-phuong* were blossoming in Vietnam, Raymond and I raced home faster than all my sisters. We were the first to see Father and Little Quang at the picture window, and beside them . . .
> Mother!

The beginning of the story made you want to find out if Ut's mother would come, and the ending gives you the answer.

Voice

Your writing should sound as though you are
- ▶ aware of your audience
- ▶ involved in the topic

Each writer has his or her own voice. Your voice is what makes your writing different from anyone else's. You should always keep in mind who your audience is so you can try to connect to them. You should care about your topic so you can make your audience care. When you care about your topic and want to share it with your readers, your enthusiasm comes through.

Take a Look

Just as Chi Hai spoke, a snowrock stung her chin. That red-haired boy darted behind the dumpster. He was laughing hard.

I tried, but I could not be a noble Dragon. Before I knew it, I was scooping up snow. My hands burned and my fingers turned red. I threw my snowrock and the laughing stopped.

In these paragraphs from *Angel Child, Dragon Child*, Michele Maria Surat helps us know that Ut is a gentle, obedient child. Surat also helps us feel Ut's anger and frustration. She can no longer put up with the teasing of the red-haired boy.

Word Choice

The words you choose should
- ▶ be precise
- ▶ be original
- ▶ help create a picture in the reader's mind

You should not repeat words too much. You should use words that are precise. For example, instead of using the word *flower*, you might use the word *rose*, which is more precise. You should use words that help the reader see what you are describing.

Take a Look

So all day I was brave, even when the children whispered behind their hands and the clock needles ticked slowly. Finally, the bell trilled. Time for home!

Surat's choice of words was very important here. Everyone has had to be brave at one time or another. It is not easy. By using the word *brave*, Surat helps us understand that Ut is having a difficult time. Do the words *clock needles* paint a better image for you than *clock hands?* Can't you just see them in your mind? Can you hear the bell trilling? Isn't that a much better word than *rang?*

Try It!

Replace words in the following sentence to create a better image.

Joe watched the snow falling.

Sentence Fluency

Your sentences should
▶ be pleasing
▶ flow
▶ have rhythm

Always read your sentences aloud. The sentences you write should flow like the sentences you use when you speak. If you listen to your sentences and those of others, you will get an idea of the styles of sentences that you like to hear and read. Writing that has only short sentences does not flow. Writing that has only long sentences can be difficult to follow. There should be a good mix of long and short sentences in your writing.

Read the sentences from *Angel Child, Dragon Child* aloud. Notice how well they fit together. Listen to how they flow. Feel the rhythm.

> "Wait," said Raymond. He grabbed part of the broken pencil. I handed him a new sheet of paper. "Now tell me about Vietnam," he said.
> Raymond scrawled my words in black squiggles. I crayoned pictures in the margins.
> When we were ready, Raymond leaned out the door. "Done!" he beamed. He waved the story like a flag.

Notice that there are some short sentences and some long ones. Also, notice that not every sentence begins with a subject.

Conventions

You should always check your
▶ spelling
▶ punctuation
▶ capitalization
▶ usage

Your writing will be easier to read if it is free of mistakes. Readers stumble over mistakes, trying to fix them in their minds before going on. That interrupts the flow of reading. Sometimes you don't know where your mistakes are. A teacher, parent, or friend can help you find the mistakes, and they can help you figure out how to fix them.

Presentation

How writing looks on a page is important. This is called **presentation.** Your written work should be neatly typed or handwritten. Writing and illustrations on a page should be pleasing to the reader.

Reading Your Writing
The traits of good writing are ideas, organization, voice, word choice, sentence fluency, conventions, and presentation. Think about the traits of good writing as you write fiction, nonfiction, and poetry. By using these traits, you will make your writing more enjoyable to your readers.

The Writing Process

Learning to write can be fun. The writing process can help. There are five parts to the writing process: prewriting, drafting, revising, editing/proofreading, and publishing. You can use them to become a better writer.

The Writing Process

You write some things quickly, such as a note to remember something. Other things, such as stories and reports, take more time and thought. To help you with all kinds of writing, use the **writing process.** It can help you organize your writing and make it the best it can be.

Prewriting

This is where it all begins. This can take a while because there is a lot of thinking and writing to do. You can use your prewriting time to

▶ think about what you want to say

▶ write down your ideas

▶ collect information

▶ think about who will read your writing

▶ decide if you are writing to entertain, to inform, to persuade, or to explain

▶ organize your ideas on paper

Drafting

This is the time to get some of your ideas down on paper. You should write quickly while your best thoughts are in your mind. You should not worry too much about spelling, punctuation, or handwriting.

Revising

During revising, you have a chance to change your writing to make it better. You can read it out loud to hear how it sounds. You can change and rearrange words, sentences, and paragraphs to make your ideas clearer. You can ask a friend to read it and tell you what is good and what could be better. You can talk to your teacher about how to make your writing better.

Editing/Proofreading

This is when you need to look at spelling and usage. If words are misspelled, or if you've used the wrong words, your readers may not be able to figure out what you are saying. You can make a list of problems that you want to look for in your writing and then read your writing over and over, checking one thing at a time.

Publishing

This is your chance to make your writing look good. Using your best handwriting or a computer, you can make a clean copy of your writing. You can add pictures, charts, or diagrams. You can bind it in a book, submit it to a magazine, or mail it if it is a letter.

Reading Your Writing

The writing process will help you organize, improve, and correct your writing. Put your writing aside between each step. This helps you take a fresh look at your writing.

How Do I Get Started?

Follow the writing process for any kind of writing. The writing process includes **prewriting, drafting, revising, editing/ proofreading,** and **publishing.** You may not always use all of these steps, but when you do, they can help you write better. Charlie uses them. Follow along as Charlie shows how she used the writing process for the writing tasks. Charlie started with the first step, which is **prewriting.**

Understanding the Task, Purpose, and Audience

Charlie's teacher asked her students to each write a paragraph describing something. Charlie had to think about and answer three questions before she got started.

1. **Task** What kind of writing are you going to do?
2. **Purpose** Will you write to entertain, to give information, to explain, or to persuade?
3. **Audience** Who will be reading your writing?

Task

This was easy for Charlie. Her teacher wanted her to write a description.

Purpose

Charlie thought about why she would write a description. She decided that her purpose was to explain.

Audience

Charlie decided that her audience would be her new pen pal, who lives in Sierra Leone. Charlie would have to think of something she knew about that he might find interesting.

Try It!

Imagine that your teacher told you to write a story about a dog. What would your task be? Who would be your audience? What would be your purpose?

Getting and Narrowing Ideas

Charlie needed to decide exactly what she would describe. She wanted to choose something that her pen pal would find interesting and that she knew well. She thought about her house, the family car, her pet dog, and her little brother. Then she asked her friends for ideas. She made a list.

my house
my family's car
my pet dog
my little brother
my face
Guy's red bicycle
Sears Tower
cornstalks on Grandpa's farm

Try It!
Imagine describing something to Charlie's pen pal in Sierra Leone. What ideas do you and your friends have about the kinds of things you might describe?

Choosing a Topic

Now that Charlie had some ideas, she had to choose one idea to write about. How did she do that? She asked herself

▶ What would my pen pal want to read about?

▶ I want to explain something, so which thing on my list do I know the most about?

▶ Which thing on my list can I describe the best?

Charlie looked over her list carefully. She thought that he had probably seen bicycles, cars, and cornstalks, so those things wouldn't be anything new to him. The Sears Tower is a tall, brown building, so Charlie thought that wouldn't be very interesting to describe. Finally, Charlie decided that because her pen pal had never seen her, she would describe her own face.

Try It!
Ask yourself the same questions Charlie asked herself. What idea would you choose from your earlier list?

Fun Fact

Sierra Leone is a country on Africa's western coast. Monkeys, chimpanzees, tigers, porcupines, antelope, and crocodiles live there.

Organizing Ideas

This part worried Charlie the most. She was very unorganized. Her desk was always a mess. She often lost her homework. She forgot where she put her shoes almost every day.

Charlie needed help organizing her ideas. Luckily, her teacher said, "Remember, you can use graphic organizers to help you organize your ideas." Charlie let out a huge sigh. Now she had somewhere to begin.

A **graphic organizer** is a diagram that helps a writer put ideas in an order that makes sense. Charlie decided to use a **web.**

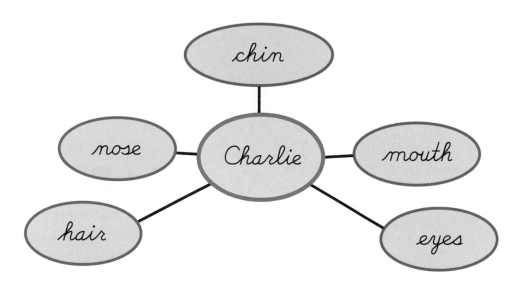

Charlie thought this was a good start, but she needed more details for a good description. She also needed to put the details in order. Charlie tried to think of other organizers.

Time Line

The next graphic organizer Charlie remembered was a time line. It looked like this:

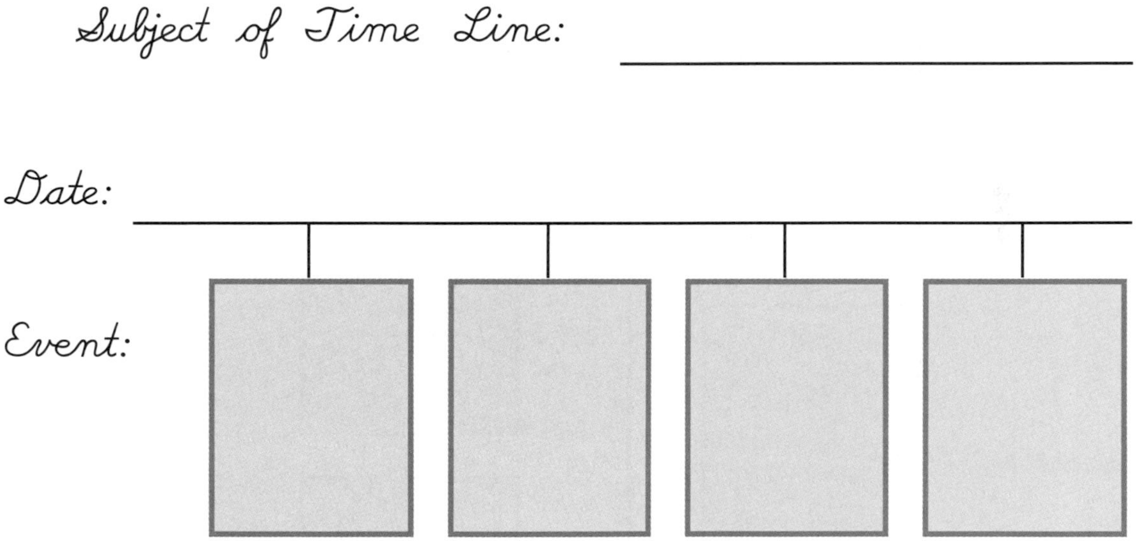

Subject of Time Line: _____

Date: _____

Event:

[ ] [ ] [ ] [ ]

Charlie knew that a time line would not work at all. A time line shows events that happened during a certain period. She could use a time line to tell about what had happened in her life, but that was not her task. She needed to describe her face.

Chain of Events

Then Charlie thought of another graphic organizer. It shows events in the order they happen.

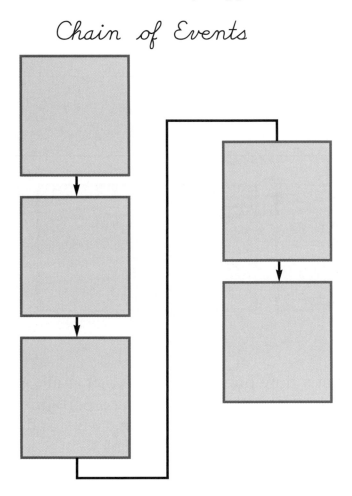

Chain of Events

Charlie was stumped. What other organizer could she use? She knew she needed to organize the details in her description. Charlie looked at her face closely in a mirror. "That's it!" she exclaimed. Charlie realized that she had looked at her face from top to bottom. She decided to organize her description the same way.

Spatial Order

Charlie came up with this graphic organizer herself. Notice that she put what she was describing, her face, at the top. Then she put details about her face in order from top to bottom in the other boxes.

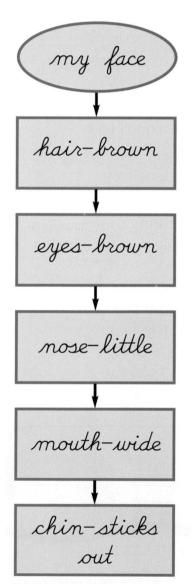

This graphic organizer helped Charlie put her ideas in an order that would be easy for her reader to follow. Charlie found out that prewriting can take a long time but that it will be very helpful when she writes her draft.

How Do I Begin to Write?

The next step in the writing process is **drafting.** In this step, Charlie used the information in her graphic organizer to write a draft. She tried to keep her audience in mind as she wrote.

Charlie knew that she had to write her thoughts down quickly. Here are some helpful hints she used to do that.

▶ Don't worry about spelling, punctuation, or handwriting.

▶ Write on every other line. This will give you room to add things later.

▶ Use abbreviations or write the sounds you hear in a word that you can't spell.

▶ Cross out or circle words that you plan to change later.

▶ Leave blanks when you can't think of a word.

Charlie looked at all the information in her graphic organizer. She wasn't sure if she should write a single paragraph or separate paragraphs for each of the boxes in her organizer. She thought that one paragraph would be enough. First, she wrote a topic sentence that told the main idea for her description.

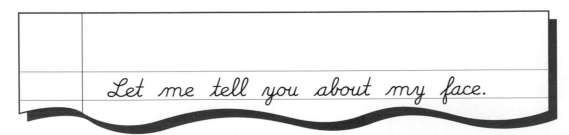

Let me tell you about my face.

Beginning to Write

Then, Charlie wrote a sentence for each detail in her graphic organizer.

Let me tell you about my face.

My hair is brown. It is strate.

My eyes are brown My friend has

blue eyes. my chin is p____y.

My nose is kind of small. My

mouth is kind of big. My feet

are huge.

Reading Your Writing
During drafting it is important to get your ideas on paper quickly. That way, you won't forget any of them.

How Can I Improve My Writing?

When you are done with your draft, it is a good idea to put it aside for a while. You might get some new ideas when you aren't thinking so hard about your writing. You make your writing better during **revising**. If you have written your draft on a computer, you may want to save each new version in a separate file.

Charlie knew that revising also takes a while. She would need to read her writing several times, looking for ways to improve it. She would also let her classmates read her writing. They might spot ways to improve her description that she may have missed. Charlie knew that these questions based on the traits of writing would also help.

Ideas
▶ Is the main idea clear?
▶ Do I stay on the topic?

Organization
▶ Do I follow the order I decided on in prewriting?

Word Choice
▶ Do I repeat some words too often?
▶ Do I use the best words to describe my face?

Sentence Fluency
▶ Do my sentences read smoothly?
▶ Do I use sentences that are too short or too long?

Voice
▶ Do I show my audience my face with words?

Staying on Topic

Charlie doesn't want her audience to become confused, so she read her description once to make sure that all of her sentences were about the topic she chose. Because Charlie is describing her face, all of her sentences should be about some part of her face. Charlie read her description to make sure that all of the sentences were about the main idea. Charlie realized that she had a sentence about her feet. Why did she put that in there? She crossed it out. She also thought of a couple of details she wanted to add.

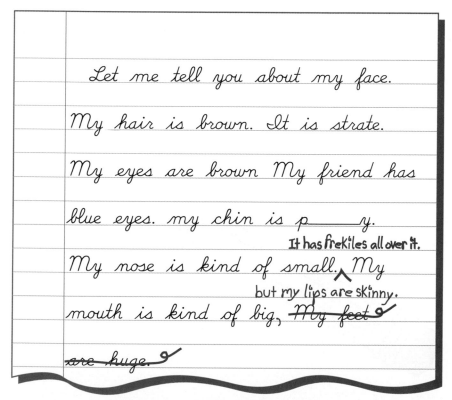

Let me tell you about my face.

My hair is brown. It is strate.

My eyes are brown My friend has

blue eyes. my chin is p_____y.

It has frekiles all over it.

My nose is kind of small. ^ My

but my lips are skinny.

mouth is kind of big, ~~My feet~~

~~are huge.~~

Try It!

Charlie has another sentence in her description that doesn't belong. Which one is it?

Coherence

Next, Charlie made sure her description was in an order that made sense. During prewriting, she had decided to describe her face from top to bottom. Charlie had thought that this way of describing her face would help her pen pal picture her.

Charlie read her description out loud and thought of two things. First, she had kept the order of her description of her face from top to bottom except for one sentence. The sentence about her chin should go last. Charlie marked the sentence to remember to move it later.

Second, Charlie noticed that some of her sentences were choppy. She thought that adding words to these sentences would make them smoother. She added the phrases *at the top of my head, below that, next,* and *at the bottom.*

Try It!

Think of three sentences that you could put together using the words *first*, *then*, and *finally*.

Notice the new changes that Charlie marked on her draft.

Let me tell you about my face. ∧
At the top of my head is

My hair is brown. It is strate. ∧
Below that

My eyes are brown ∧ ~~My friend has~~
Next is

~~blue eyes.~~ my chin is p_____y.

My ∧ nose. ~~is kind of small.~~ ∧ My
small   *It has frekiles all over it.*

mouth is kind of big. ~~My feet~~
but my lips are skinny.

~~are huge.~~ ∧
At the bottom is my chin.

Adding Variety

Charlie realized that writing requires a lot of work to keep readers interested. To keep readers interested, you must have some variety. If you don't have variety, your readers will get bored. If you have too much variety, your readers will not enjoy your writing. You can add variety to your writing by

▶ using specific words to create a clear picture

▶ varying sentence length—use some short and some long sentences

▶ taking out extra words

▶ varying the beginnings of sentences

▶ beginning a paragraph with a question

Because her pen pal had never seen Charlie, she had to *show* him what she looks like with her words, not just tell him. She would need to choose words that would create a clear and vivid picture for him. In her draft, Charlie had said that she had brown hair. Charlie thought about this again. "Well, there are many different colors of brown hair. There are dark brown, light brown, and red-brown." Charlie decided that she would need to be more specific if she wanted her pen pal to really be able to "see" her hair.

Try It!
You have seen Charlie. What words could she add to help her pen pal see her hair in his mind?

Making Your Writing More Interesting

Charlie decided that she could make her description better. She tried adding new words, taking out words, and combining sentences.

Charlie asked her friend Paul to read her description. He said nice things about her word choices and her use of variety in her sentences. He thought her beginning would be better if she began with a question.

Do you wonder what I look like? ~~Let me tell you about my face.~~ At the top of my head is

My hair is ^{red-}brown. ~~And is~~ ^{and} strate. ^{Below that}

My eyes are brown. ^{Next is} ~~My friend has blue eyes.~~ my chin is p____y.

My ^{small} nose. ~~is kind of small.~~ ^{It has frekiles all over it.} My mouth is kind of big, ~~My feet~~ ^{but my lips are skinny.}

At the bottom is my chin. ~~are huge.~~

Conferencing

Your classmates can be a big help during the revising process. They can give you one last, fresh look at your writing. Having a **conference** with one or more classmates is a way to find out what is good in your writing and what can be better.

There are two roles in a conference: writers and listeners. During a conference, the writer asks other students to listen to and comment on his or her writing.

Here are some things that a writer and listeners do in a conference.

During a conference, the writer	**The writer needs to remember that**
▶ reads his or her work out loud	▶ listeners are trying to help
▶ records others' comments	▶ most writing can be improved
▶ decides which comments to use	▶ it is good to get feedback from others
▶ marks his or her paper for revisions	▶ he or she will make the final decisions

During a conference, listeners	**The listeners need to remember**
▶ point out things they liked	▶ to respect the writer's hard work
▶ point out places they had trouble understanding	▶ that everybody wants to hear good things about their writing
	▶ to listen carefully and be polite

Try It!
Ask a couple of friends to listen to something that you have written. Ask them to tell one thing they liked and one thing they think could be better.

Everyone must remember to be helpful, not hurtful, during conferences. Here are some rules that will help conferences go smoothly.

Rules for Good Conferences

1. Listen quietly when others are speaking.
2. Think carefully before you say anything about another person's work.
3. Be specific.
4. Tell something you like before you tell what can be improved.
5. Discuss quietly so you do not disturb others who are working nearby.

Reading Your Writing

Writing takes a lot of time and effort. Sometimes your writing is not clear to your audience. Revising, staying on topic, adding variety, and conferencing are all ways that you can make your writing better. It is also a good idea to have others listen to and comment on your writing.

Fun Fact

A conference is a meeting between two or more people to discuss something. The word *conference* has been in use for about 500 years!

How Do I Edit/ Proofread My Writing?

The next step is **editing/proofreading,** where you will look at the conventions of writing. The conventions of writing are spelling, grammar, usage, and mechanics. You will correct misspelled words. You will look for punctuation errors. You will make sure that you have used capital letters where they belong. You will make sure that your sentences are complete and that they read smoothly.

Using Proofreading Marks

Charlie planned to use special marks on her paper to show where she needed to make corrections. These are called **proofreading marks.** Charlie liked using them because they saved her time and they showed her what needed to be rewritten. Here are the proofreading marks that Charlie knows.

¶ Indent the paragraph.   ⹀ Make a capital letter.

∧ Add something.   ⓢᴘ Check spelling.

ꝰ Take out something.   ⊙ Add a period.

/ Make a small letter.

> **Try It!**
> Look at Charlie's revised description on page 31. What proofreading marks do you think she will need to use?

Using an Editing/Proofreading Checklist

Charlie's teacher helped her make an editing/proofreading checklist. That way she wouldn't forget to check for spelling errors, sentence fragments, or missing punctuation.

▶ Each sentence begins with a capital letter.

▶ Each sentence ends with the correct punctuation.

▶ Commas are used in compound sentences.

▶ Each sentence is complete.

▶ Each word is spelled correctly.

▶ The paragraph is indented.

Here is Charlie's edited paragraph.

Do you wonder what I look like? At the top of my head is ~~Let me tell you about my face.~~

My hair It is red- brown. ~~It is~~ and SP ⟨strate⟩ Below that,

My eyes are brown. Next is ~~My friend has~~

~~blue eyes.~~ my chin is pointy.

It has SP ⟨frekiles⟩ all over it.

My small nose. ~~is kind of small.~~ My

mouth is kind of big, but my lips are skinny. ~~My feet~~

At the bottom is my chin.
~~are huge.~~

Good Presentation

Because Charlie's teacher wants her to hand in her letter to her pen pal, she will prepare a neat copy that will be easy to read. She will use her best handwriting. Then she will check this copy against her edited copy to make sure she has put in all of the changes she wanted to make.

Do you wonder what I look like? At the top of my head is my hair. It is red-brown and straight. Below that, my eyes are brown. Next is my small nose. It has freckles all over it. My mouth is kind of big, but my lips are skinny. At the bottom is my chin. My chin is pointy.

Editing/Proofreading on a Computer

If you have written your paper on a computer, you may want to use the spelling and grammar tools to edit/proofread it. You should still read your printed copy for errors.

Here are some tips.

To insert punctuation or words	Move the cursor to the correct place and type in the change.
To check spelling	Click on the spell-check button.
To indent paragraphs	Place the cursor in front of the first word in the paragraph, then press the tab key.
To move text	Select the text to be moved, then click the cut button. Move the cursor to where you want the text, then click on the paste button.

WARNING: Spell checkers will not catch all spelling mistakes. You may use the wrong word but spell it correctly. Spell checkers won't catch this type of mistake.

Take a Look

A spell checker missed the two mistakes in the following sentence. Do you know why?

should be **to** ▶ James went too the story. ◀ should be **store**

How Can I Share My Writing?

The last step in the writing process is **publishing.** At this stage, you are ready to share your writing with others. If you haven't already, you need to make a clean copy in your best handwriting or on the computer. The form in which you choose to publish your writing depends on what kind of writing it is and who your audience is. You should choose the best way to share what you have done for the audience that you have chosen.

Ways to Publish

If your writing is a story, you could make it a book and put it in the reading center.

How to Make a Book	
1. Fold some 8 1/2 × 11-inch paper in half.	**4.** Draw pictures or add charts, tables, or diagrams.
2. Staple it in the middle.	**5.** Put a construction paper cover on it.
3. Write your story on the pages.	**6.** Write the title and your name on the cover.

If it is a letter, you should mail it.

If it is a play or a story, you could act it out.

If it is a description, you could illustrate it and put it on a bulletin board. That is what Charlie has decided for now. Later, she will include it in a letter to her pen pal. Then she will mail it to him.

To Publish or Not to Publish

You may not publish every piece of writing you create. To decide if you want to publish something, ask yourself,

▶ Is this my best piece?

▶ Should I publish this type of writing?

▶ Who will read my writing?

▶ Have I revised it to make it better?

▶ Have I proofread it carefully?

You will also want to think about what more you can do with your piece of writing. Perhaps you can add something. What you choose to add will depend again on what kind of writing it is, the way you plan to publish, and your audience. Here are some things you might add.

▶ Photographs can be used in a description, a story about yourself, or a biography. Remember to write captions.

▶ A chart or a graph can be used in an article.

▶ A diagram can be used if you have explained how to make something or how something works.

▶ Drawings or diagrams can be used to illustrate a point or add interest to your writing.

Try It!
Think about a piece of writing you have done recently. To publish this piece, what could you add to it?

Using Charts, Tables, and Diagrams

You may choose to add charts, tables, and diagrams to your writing. Charts and tables can show a lot of information in a small amount of space. Diagrams can clearly illustrate something you are explaining. You might want to use one of these in your writing if it will help your reader understand what you are saying.

Using a Chart or Table

If you have similar information about several items in your writing, you can put it in an easy-to-read chart or table.

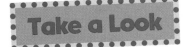

Favorite Cafeteria Lunch

	Pizza	Hamburger	Taco
First Grade	X		
Second Grade			X
Third Grade		X	
Fourth Grade			X
Fifth Grade		X	

Try It!

What do you know by studying the table above? You can create charts and tables by drawing them, or you can make them on a computer.

Using a Diagram

A diagram can be helpful if you are explaining something. For example, if you are describing the parts of a bicycle, you could put a diagram of a bike in your paper and label it. This would make what you are saying clearer. It can also add information to what you have written. It would be boring to tell the location of all the bike parts. With a diagram, that information is easy to see.

Take a Look

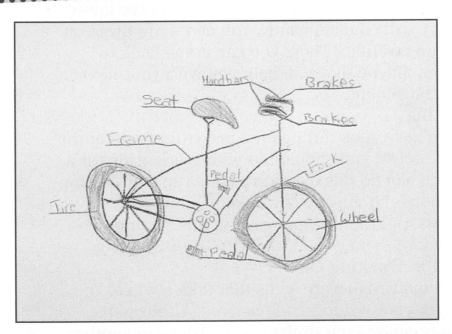

Try It!
Imagine that you are describing how to build a kite. Would you describe it with a chart, table, or diagram? Why?

Keeping a Portfolio

The more you write, the more ideas you will have. Because you won't write about every idea you have right away, you need a place to keep them. A **portfolio** is a place to keep ideas and bits of information that you might use someday in your writing. You can divide your portfolio into five sections.

1. **Getting Ideas**

   Ideas come from many different places and experiences. You might get an idea from a dream, from talking to a friend, or from a place you have visited. You probably have many more ideas than you have time to write. Save these ideas. You never know when they will come in handy. You can write these on a page in a portfolio. Then, you can come back to them later. Maybe they will help you with your next writing assignment.

2. **Prewriting**

   After you have gone through the prewriting step of the writing process, you should put your work aside for a while. You can do this by putting it in a special section of your portfolio. Also, you can keep copies of your notes, lists, or graphic organizers in this section to keep track of them.

3. **Pieces I'm Working On**

   Drafting and revising are steps that take a while. You should put your writing aside between these steps. You can organize your drafts and revisions in another section of your portfolio. You may want to put them in order by date. That way, you can keep track of the changes you make to your writing.

4. Finished Writing

In this section, you can save all of your completed writing pieces or just the best ones that you want to save.

5. Word List

Are there some words that you always have trouble spelling? Do you sometimes hear a new word that you really like? You can keep a list of words that you use often in this section of your portfolio. That way, you can easily find them when you want to use them.

Making a Portfolio

You will need a three-ring notebook and dividers with pockets.

How to make the pocket dividers

1. Cut a piece of heavy paper that is 9 inches wide and 14 inches long.

2. Fold the paper up 4 1/2 inches to make a pocket. Staple the paper along the edges.

3. Punch three holes in each pocket divider. Put the dividers in the notebook. Put some paper in it, too.

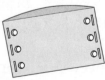

How Does It All Work Together?

Now that Charlie had worked through all of the steps of the writing process, she felt much more prepared for her next writing assignment. Her teacher asked her to write about her pet.

Prewriting Task, Audience, and Purpose

Charlie's task was to write about her pet. She has a cat named Kat. She decided that her audience would be her classmates. Her purpose would be to either inform or entertain.

Getting and Narrowing Ideas

Charlie thought about Kat. She made the following list with the help of her classmates.

how she behaves
how she looks
how to care for her
where did you get her

Charlie asked herself, "What would my classmates be interested in reading about Kat?"

She chose the first three ideas on the list. Charlie decided to write a paper that would inform her readers.

Organizing Ideas

Here is the graphic organizer that Charlie used.

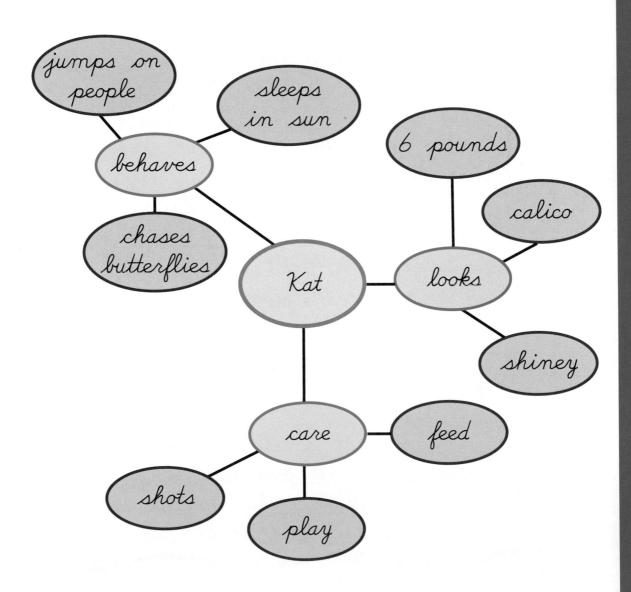

Drafting

Charlie used her graphic organizer to write this draft about Kat.

My pet is a cat named Kat. She is a calico cat. She has white, black, and orange fur. That makes her a calico cat. She takes good care of her fur so it is very shiney. She w_____ about six pounds.

Kat spends most of her day sleeping in the sun. When I take her outside, she chases butterflies. She also jumps on the backs of people who walk past her favrit tree.

I love Kat so I take very good care of her. I feed her. I play with her. I take her to the vet for a checkup and shots.

Charlie put her draft in her portfolio when she was done. She would revise it later.

Revising

Charlie read her draft several times. First, she took out extra information. Charlie also added words to make some of her sentences more interesting.

My pet is a ^pretty cat named Kat. She is a calico cat. ~~She has~~ ^with white, black, and orange fur. ~~That makes her a calico cat.~~ She takes good care of her fur so it is very shiney. She w_____ about six pounds.

~~sometimes she is active and sometimes she isn't~~
Kat spends most of her day sleeping in the sun. When I take her outside, she chases butterflies. She also jumps on the backs of people who walk past her favrit tree.

I love Kat so I take very good care of her. ^Before school I feed her. ^After school I play with her. ^Once a year I take her to the vet for a checkup and shots.

Editing/Proofreading

Charlie used her editing/proofreading checklist. She looked for misspelled words and incorrect punctuation. Charlie noticed some mistakes she had made. She marked them with proofreading marks.

Fun Fact

Avi, who has written many books, including *Poppy*, has a learning disability that makes spelling difficult for him. It's a good thing he keeps writing anyway, because he has wonderful stories to tell.

> My pet is a ^pretty^ cat named Kat. ~~She is a calico cat.~~ ~~She has~~ ^with^ white, black, and orange fur. ~~That makes her a calico cat.~~ She takes good care of her fur, so it is very (shiney) *sp?* She w_eighs_ about six pounds.
>
> ~~sometimes she is active and sometimes she isn't~~ Kat spends most of her day sleeping in the sun. When I take her outside, she chases butterflies. She also jumps on the backs of people who walk past her (favrit) *sp? favorite* tree.
>
> I love Kat, so I take very good care of her. ^Before school^ I feed her. ^After school^ I play with her. ^Once a year^ I take her to the vet for a checkup and shots.

Publishing

Charlie was ready to share her writing with the class. She thought about the best way to do that. She thought it would be fun to make a cat-shaped book. She wrote a couple of sentences on each page in her best handwriting. Then she drew pictures of Kat to go with the words. Finally, Charlie checked her book against her edited paragraphs to make sure she hadn't missed anything.

> My pet is a pretty cat named Kat. She is a calico cat with white, black, and orange fur. She takes good

> care of her fur, so it is very shiny. She weighs about six pounds.
>
> Sometimes she is active

Reading Your Writing

Following all of the parts of the writing process will make your writing better. The steps will help you get and narrow ideas and organize your thoughts. They will also help you change, correct, and add to your writing to make it more interesting and easy to read. When you're ready to share your writing with others, the writing process will help you get it ready to publish.

Forms of Writing

This is the part of the Handbook where you can find out how to write letters, reports, stories, descriptions, poetry, and much more. All the different kinds of writing you do are included here, plus some other kinds you may not have tried yet. Are you ready? Then let's get started.

Personal Writing

Do you make lists to remind yourself to do things? Do you write notes to your friends? These are examples of personal writing. Look on the next page for more kinds of personal writing you can do.

Lists

A **list** is a group of related names, things, or actions. You have probably seen lists for grocery shopping, students in a class, or things a child wants for a birthday gift. The words on a particular list are all about the same subject.

Here are three different kinds of lists.

Grocery List
milk
eggs
butter
oranges
bread
peanut butter

Mrs. Miller's 3rd Grade Class	
Kayla	Mark
Emily	Tyler
Megan	Justin
Julia	Brian
Nikkie	Juan
Amber	David
Mary	Alex
Lauren	Jamal
Diana	Paul

Birthday Wish List
watch
backpack
soccer ball
board game

Reasons for Lists

People make lists for many different reasons. You can make lists to help you remember things, to give more information to others, or to get ideas for writing. There are many different kinds of lists.

Suppose you are planning a birthday party. Writing lists can help you in three ways.

1. **Lists to help remember things**
   List of things to eat (pizza, juice, pretzels)
   List of things to do at your party (play games, face painting, open presents)
   List of friends to invite to your party (Emily, Tyler, Julia, Juan, Mary, Diana, Paul, Alex)

2. **List to give information to others**
   List of things to write on the invitations (date, time, and place of party)

3. **List to get ideas for writing**
   List of funny things that happened at your party (I wore all the bows from my presents; the dog ran off with the last piece of pizza.)

Reading Your Writing

Lists are a good way to help you remember things. You can use lists for lots of different things, including grocery lists and information to include on a party invitation. Make sure you include everything on your list, so your reader will have all of the information they need.

Journals

Wouldn't it be nice to write whatever you want and not worry about how it looks or sounds? That's what you can do in a **journal.** It's a place where you can write about anything, in any way you want!

You can write about things that happen to you and how you feel about them. You can write about things you've done and things you want to do. You can write about movies you see or books you read. Your journal is your very own place to write your thoughts about everything.

Soccer practice starts on Tuesday and Cody can hardly wait. He wrote about his favorite sport in his journal.

Take a Look

September 1

It's so fun to play soccer! It's the best to be the goalie because you can catch the ball and you can kick it to your teammates. You don't have to do as much work, like running and never getting the ball.

Try It!

Here are some things you could write about in your journal.

▶ camping with your family

▶ riding a roller coaster

▶ a funny thing that happened at school

▶ a visit to a famous place

▶ a book you really liked

More About Journals

People who write books, magazines, and newspaper stories need lots of ideas for their writing. Many authors write in journals. Then they use ideas from their journals to write stories.

Tips for Writing in Journals

▶ Don't worry about spelling, punctuation, or neat handwriting. As long as you can read it, that's what matters.

▶ You can draw in your journal. Sometimes a drawing will give you a great idea for a story.

▶ Try to write in your journal every day. The more you write, the more ideas you will have.

Fun Fact

The artist who painted the *Mona Lisa* also wrote and drew in journals. Leonardo da Vinci studied science and art. He drew plans for a flying machine 400 years before the first airplane flew.

Reading Your Writing

Writing in a journal is a good way to keep track of ideas for your writing. You can write down ideas you don't want to forget and write about them later. The more ideas you have to choose from, the easier it will be to pick a topic that will interest your readers.

Learning Logs

A **learning log** is a place where you write about something you are studying. For example, if you are doing a science experiment, you watch for changes. You can record those changes in a learning log.

Learning logs can be used for any subject you are studying. You can use charts or drawings in your learning log to help keep track of what you are studying.

Arthur wanted to grow "rock candy." His mother heated a cup of water. Arthur stirred lots of sugar into the jar of hot water. When sugar stayed on the bottom, he stopped.

Arthur tied a paper clip to one end of a piece of string and a pencil to the other. He dropped the paper clip into the sugar water and put the pencil over the top of the jar.

Arthur wrote in his learning log whenever he saw changes. Here is part of his learning log.

> ### Making Rock Candy
>
> November 1
>
> Today I mixed lots of sugar in hot water. I hope my rock candy will grow soon.
>
> November 7
>
> There is something on the string! It looks kind of like ice.
>
> November 10
>
> The rock candy is growing bigger. I can't wait to try it!

Dad helped me hang the tray from a tree. We hope it will keep the squirrels away.

The birds came back! I saw lots of sparrows and finches. There was even a red cardinal!

A squirrel got up on the feeder today. It chased away all the birds!

Today I saw a sparrow. It's the first bird to eat at the feeder!

Fun Fact

Scientists use something like a learning log when they study a problem. It's called the scientific method. First they take a problem and state a possible answer. Then scientists keep a log of what they see and do. Finally, they read their logs and see if their possible answer was right or wrong.

When you need an idea for writing, read your learning log. The things in your log can be used to write a letter, story, or class report. You record things in the order they happened, so you will be able to write in a clear, orderly way that will be easy for your readers to understand and follow.

Notes and Cards

There are many different kinds of notes and cards. You have probably seen card racks in stores. They have notes and cards for every kind of holiday and event you can think of. There are even cards to wish someone a "Happy Groundhog Day"!

You can buy a card or print one out on a computer. You can also make a card yourself. Add your own personal message and you are ready to send a note or card.

Birthday Card

A birthday card is sent to wish someone a "Happy Birthday." You usually send them before the person's birthday. However, there are special *belated* birthday cards in case you remember the birthday after it is over. Here is the message Eric wrote in a birthday card he made for his grandma.

Take a Look

Happy Birthday!

Grandma,

Happy Birthday! I wish I could give you a big hug on your birthday. We will see you at Thanksgiving.

Love,

Eric

Get-Well Card

A **get-well card** is sent to cheer up someone who is sick or hurt. Jessica made her friend Ben a get-well card when he was sick with a cold.

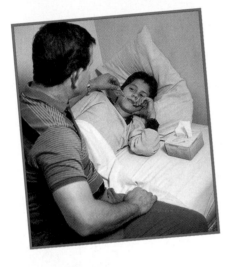

Hi Ben,
    We missed you at baseball practice! Here is a joke to make you feel better. What animal keeps the best time? A watch dog!
See you soon,
Jessica

Get well soon!

Invitation

An **invitation** is a card that asks someone to come somewhere. It should tell the date and time to come and the address where people should go.

You're Invited!

Dayton, Ohio 43012

Come help us celebrate Danny's 9th birthday!

Date: Saturday, February 5
Time: 2:00 p.m.
Address: 777 Luby Lane
               Dayton, Ohio 43012

Thank-You Note

Write a **thank-you note** when you want to thank someone for giving you something or for doing something nice for you. The thank-you note has special information in the *body*. It says thank you and tells why you are thanking the person. Your thank-you note must also have a *greeting*, *closing*, and *signature*.

Brad wrote a thank-you note to his aunt.

Greeting ▶ Dear Aunt Jane,

Body ▶   Thank you for letting me come to visit you. I had a great time! I really like the haircut you gave me. The kids in my class think it's really cool.

Closing ▶   Love,

Signature ▶   Brad

Try It!

Which kind of note or card would you send for each event below?

▶ You are having a Valentine's Day party.

▶ Your uncle broke his arm.

▶ Your grandpa sent you a basketball.

▶ Your friend is having a birthday soon.

Tips for Writing Notes and Cards

▶ Make sure you have spelled the person's name correctly.

▶ Be friendly and polite.

▶ Put commas after the name of the person in the *greeting* and after the *closing: Dear Uncle Bob, Sincerely,*

▶ Decorate your notes and cards with your own drawings and designs.

▶ Remember to include the date, time, and address on invitations.

▶ When you write a thank-you note, be sure to mention the specific gift or assistance you received from the person.

Reading Your Writing

Notes and cards are written for special occasions like birthdays, to let someone know you hope they feel better soon, to invite someone somewhere, and to thank someone.

When writing notes and cards, be sure to be friendly and polite. Make sure you have included all of the parts of the note or card you are sending. If you leave something out, your reader will be confused.

Friendly Letters

A **friendly letter** is a letter you write to a relative or a friend. It's also a letter you write to someone you would like to get to know. Friendly letters can be written to a pen pal. They can also be written to a favorite author, actor, actress, or athlete.

Friendly letters help you share news, stories, and thoughts. They help you start or continue friendships with people who live far away.

The Parts of a Friendly Letter

Heading

The *heading* is your address and the date. The heading goes in the upper right corner of the friendly letter.

Greeting

The *greeting* tells who will receive the letter. Many greetings begin with *Dear*, but you can also use words like *Hi*. Put a comma after the person's name.

Body

The *body* is the main part of the letter. This is where you write the news, stories, and thoughts you want to tell.

Closing

The *closing* lets the person know you are ending the letter. Words like *Love*, *Your friend*, and *Sincerely* are often used as closings. Be sure to put a comma after the closing.

Signature

The *signature* is your name.

Grace just moved to Montana. Her best friend Allie still lives in Kansas. Grace wrote a friendly letter to Allie.

Heading ▶

853 Mountain View Lane
Glen Echo, Montana 20812
September 8, 2003

Greeting ▶ Dear Allie,

Body ▶   Today was the first day of school. It's really hard to be the new kid in class. One girl named Mandy was really nice. She has red hair like you!

You know what's weird? It already snowed! It didn't snow here in town, just on top of the mountains. Then it melted.

I haven't seen any moose or grizzly bears yet. I hope I don't see a grizzly bear.

Guess what! They have soccer here too! Dad said that I could play. I wish you could be on my team again.

I miss you so much. Please write to me soon.

Closing ▶

Love,

Signature ▶

Grace

Addressing the Envelope

There are three lines to each **address**.

1. The *person's name* is on the first line. Use the person's first and last names. Be sure to capitalize the first letter of each name.

2. The *house number* and *street name* go on the second line. If there is an *apartment number*, add it after the street name. Capitalize the first letter of each word in the street name.

3. The *city*, *state*, and *zip code* go on the third line. Capitalize the names of the city and the state. Put a comma between the city and the state. Put a space between the state and the zip code.

Tips for Addressing an Envelope

▶ Put your address in the upper left corner of the envelope.

▶ Put the address of the person you are writing in the middle of the envelope.

▶ Put a stamp in the upper right corner of the envelope.

Here is the envelope Grace addressed to her friend Allie.

Take a Look

Grace Anderson ◀ **Name**
853 Mountain View Lane ◀ **Number, Street**
Glen Echo, Montana 20812 ◀ **City, State, Zip**

Stamp ▲

Name ▶ Allie Jenkins
Number, Street ▶ 3458 Sunflower Street
City, State, Zip ▶ Salina, Kansas 67401

Tips for Writing Friendly Letters

Prewriting Make a Plan

▶ List things you've done since you last wrote to the person.

▶ Read your journal for writing ideas.

Drafting Get Your Thoughts on Paper

▶ Write your letter. Use your list of new things.

▶ Write as if you were talking to the person.

▶ Write the body of your letter. Then add the other parts: heading, closing, and signature.

Revising Be Sure It Makes Sense

▶ **Organization** Put all the sentences about the same thing in the same paragraph. Add a topic sentence at the beginning.

▶ **Sentence Fluency** Are sentences smooth and easy to read?

▶ **Voice** Read your letter out loud. Does it sound like you are talking to a friend?

Editing/Proofreading Look Closely at the Details

▶ **Conventions** Look for spelling mistakes in your letter. Be sure your friend's name is spelled correctly! Make sure your friend's name and other proper nouns are capitalized. Check for correct punctuation.

Publishing Get Your Letter Ready to Mail

▶ **Presentation** Type or write a neat final copy of your letter. Make sure it looks nice and is easy to read.

▶ Address the envelope. Put a stamp on it. Now, mail your letter!

Business Letters

A **business letter** is a serious letter you write to someone at an organization or company for one special reason. It isn't a friendly letter filled with stories and jokes. Some business letters ask that something wrong be fixed. Others request information.

Here are three kinds of business letters and reasons to write them.

1. **A Letter of Complaint** states a problem you have with a product or service offered by a company and asks the reader to fix the problem.

   Suppose you order a paper airplane book. The book company sends you a paper doll book instead. You write a letter of complaint to the book company. You state the problem and ask the company to send the right book.

2. **A Letter of Concern** is written when people are concerned or interested in the same issue. It could be about an issue in your school, your neighborhood, or your city. It's a way of calling the attention of many people to a concern or other idea.

   For example, without special curbs, it's hard for people in wheelchairs to cross streets. You could write a letter to express your concern. You could send it to the newspaper editor to be printed in the paper. If others agree with your concern, your town will begin thinking about making curbs with wheelchair access.

3. **A Letter of Request** asks the reader to send information. You think you can break the world record for the most dominoes stacked. You write a letter of request for information on how to get into *The Guinness Book of World Records*.

Checklist for Business Letters

Use this checklist to make sure your business letters are written properly.

▶ Be serious about your letter. Your reader will be serious about it too.

▶ Be polite. Ask, and don't make demands.

▶ Keep it short. It's easier to keep your reader's interest with a short letter.

▶ "Stick to business." Stay on the subject and you won't lose your reader.

▶ Thank the reader for his or her help.

Try It!
Pick the two letters that are business letters.

▶ A letter to your cousin Bill about coming for a visit

▶ A letter to a toy company asking for its price list

▶ A letter to your friend Liz about the fun you had at the county fair

▶ A letter to a farmer thanking him for having your class visit for a field trip

▶ A letter to the city pointing out the need for more playgrounds in the city parks

Parts of a Business Letter

Heading

The heading is your address and the date. The heading in a business letter goes in the upper left corner of the letter.

Inside Address

The inside address is the name and address of the person you are writing. The inside address goes between the heading and the greeting. If the person has a title, put a comma after the name and then write the title.

Ms. Carolyn Greenfield, Museum Director

Greeting

The greeting of a business letter is followed by a colon.

Dear Ms. Greenfield:

Body

The body is the main part of the business letter. This is where you write about the problem or ask for information. You don't indent the paragraphs in the body of a business letter.

Closing

The closing goes on the left side of the page, after the body. Words and phrases such as *Sincerely, Sincerely yours,* and *Yours truly* are often used as closings for a business letter. Put a comma after the closing.

Signature

The signature is your handwritten name. If you are using a computer, type your full name four lines below the closing. Sign your name above your typed name.

Jose likes to play with dominoes. His mom read *Guinness World Records 2000*. She told Jose about Edwin Sirko's record of 545 dominoes stacked on one upright domino. Jose practiced stacking dominoes until he broke Edwin's record. Jose wrote a **business letter** to Guinness Media, Inc., about his record.

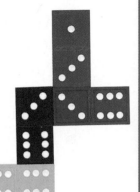

Take a Look

174 Cactus Court
Winslow, Arizona 86047
January 18, 2001   ◀ **Heading**

Guinness Media, Inc.   ◀ **Inside Address**
6 Landmark Square
Stamford, Connecticut 06901

Greetings: ◀ **Greeting**
I beat the world record for stacked dominoes. I stacked 552   ◀ **Body**
dominoes on top of one standing domino. That is seven more than
Edwin Sirko stacked. I want to be in <u>The Guinness Book of
World Records.</u>

Please send me the guidelines of how to get my record into your
book. I would also like a certificate showing that I broke a record.
Thank you very much.
Yours truly,   ◀ **Closing**
Jose Sanchez   ◀ **Signature**
Jose Sanchez

Checklist for Addressing Envelopes

▶ Write your address in the upper left corner of the envelope.

▶ Put the address of the person, company, or organization you wrote to in the middle of the envelope.

▶ Put a stamp in the upper right corner of the envelope.

Take a Look

Here is the envelope Jose addressed to the Guinness Media Company.

Jose Sanchez
174 Cactus Court
Winslow, Arizona 86047   ◀ **Your Address**

Stamp ▲

Company Address ▶ Guinness Media, Inc.
6 Landmark Square
Stamford, Connecticut 06901

Folding Letters

Fold your letter into three parts. Put your letter into the addressed envelope. Seal the envelope and mail your business letter!

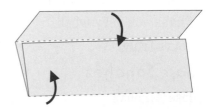

Tips for Writing Business Letters

Prewriting Make a Plan

▶ List things you could write about in a business letter. These should include questions, concerns, and complaints.

▶ Read the "Checklist for Business Letters" to help plan your letter.

Drafting Get Your Thoughts on Paper

▶ Write your letter. Use your list to help you "stick to business."

▶ Don't worry about neatness or mistakes now. You can make corrections later.

▶ Write the body, and then add the other parts of the letter. Don't forget that a business letter has an inside address.

Revising Be Sure It Makes Sense

▶ **Organization** Make sure you stated the problem, request, or concern, asked for help, and then thanked the reader.

▶ **Voice** Read your letter out loud. It should sound like talking to a grownup you respect. It should be clear and polite.

Editing/Proofreading Look Closely at the Details

▶ **Conventions** Check for mistakes with capitalization. Be sure to capitalize a person's name and title. Don't use exclamation points in a business letter.

Publishing Get Your Letter Ready to Mail

▶ **Presentation** Write or type a neat final copy of your letter. Write your signature neatly. Address the envelope. Add a stamp. Now, mail your business letter!

Expository Writing

Expository writing does two things. It explains how to do something, or it gives information about something.

Suppose you wrote a report about your favorite animal. Suppose you wrote directions explaining how to make your favorite sandwich. Both are examples of expository writing.

Summaries

A **summary** is a short way to explain what you have learned about a piece of writing. You might write a summary after you have read a book, encyclopedia article, or news story or listened to someone else read. A summary should include the main idea and other important ideas of the writing.

Take a Look

Paul read the following part of the magazine article "Kids Did It! In Business" by Judith E. Rinard.

> When Marc Wright lays his cards on the table, he has quite a few. Marc owns his own greeting card company, called Kiddie Cards. He started the company four years ago when he was just 6. "I wanted to make extra money," says Marc, of Windsor, Ontario, in Canada. "One day I drew a picture. My mom suggested I put it on a greeting card." Marc did, and his company was launched.
>
> At first Marc made and sold his own cards, going from door to door. The cards really caught on, and people wanted more. "So I hired friends to help," he says. About 20 young artists ages 5 to 13 now work for Marc. He pays them 25 cents a card and sells the cards for about $1. He donates 10 percent of his profits to a children's charity.
>
> Marc's business has earned up to $3,000 a year and now includes mail orders worldwide. The best part of the business? "Being able to do things like take my mom on a vacation to Walt Disney World," says Marc.

Try It!

What do you think the main idea is? What other important ideas would you put in a summary?

Take a Look

Here is the summary Paul wrote.

> Marc Wright started his own ◀ **Main idea**
> card company four years ago. He
> is ten years old. He lives in ◀ **Additional Facts**
> Canada. He has 20 young people
> working for him. He gives part
> of his profits to charity. He
> earned $3,000 in one year.

Notice how Paul put the main idea in his first sentence. He included five other ideas that he thought were important. Everything Paul wrote about is in the original article. He did not give his opinion. He did not ask any questions. He did not give any new information that was not in the article.

Remember What's Important

Sometimes it is difficult to figure out what the main idea and other important ideas are. You may need to reread two or three times. The things you remember will probably be the most important. You may also get an idea from the title.

Amphibians were the first **vertebrates** (animals with a backbone) to leave the water and start living on land. They did this some three hundred million years ago. To this class of animals belong the frogs, toads, salamanders, and newts.

Frogs and toads belong to the order of **Anura.** They can be identified by a chubby body and bulging eyes.

In some species, eardrums are easily distinguishable behind the eyes.

Most frogs and toads, like other amphibians, spend part of their lives in the water and part out of it.

Which of these sentences should not be in a summary?

Frogs and toads are amphibians.
They spend part of their time in water and part on land.
Salamanders are amphibians too.
Frogs and toads are slimy.

Reading Your Writing
A summary is a quick look at a longer piece of writing. It should tell your reader what the piece is about, without giving too much away. It should be brief and to the point. Be sure to use your own words.

Tips for Writing a Summary

Prewriting Make a Plan

▶ Read the piece of writing carefully.

▶ Write down phrases to answer these questions:
Who or what was the subject of the book or article?
What was the main idea about the subject?
What else is important to my audience?

Drafting Get Your Thoughts on Paper

▶ Write your summary using your notes.

▶ Add any ideas you may get as you're writing.

▶ Use your own words. Do not copy from what you're reading.

Revising Be Sure It Makes Sense

▶ **Ideas** Check your prewriting notes. Did you include everything? Did you get the main idea?

▶ **Organization** Get rid of any information that you didn't get from the article.

Editing/Proofreading Look Closely at the Details

▶ **Conventions** Proofread your summary to check for spelling.

▶ **Conventions** Were there any words you couldn't think of that you should fill in now?

▶ **Conventions** Did you indent your paragraph?

Publishing Get Ready to Share Your Summary

▶ **Presentation** Write a neat copy. Is it clear and easy to read?

Responding to Fiction

Fiction, stories that are made up, has characters, action, setting, and ideas. When you read stories, you try to understand what they are about. You try to understand the roles of the various characters and why they acted as they did. When you write about stories, you are showing what you understand. You are also helping readers have a better understanding of a story.

Try It!

Think of a book you have read.

▶ Do you understand why the characters acted as they did?

▶ When and where did the story take place? Was that a good setting or not?

▶ What happened in the story?

▶ What did you think about the ideas in the story?

▶ What did the writer want you to learn from the story?

Creating a Web

There are many ways to respond to fiction. Lainey just finished reading *Aunt Flossie's Hats (and Crab Cakes Later)* by Elizabeth Fitzgerald Howard. Lainey decided to respond to a character. She really liked Aunt Flossie. She wished she had an aunt like Flossie. She thought about why she wanted an aunt like Flossie. She made this web to organize her ideas.

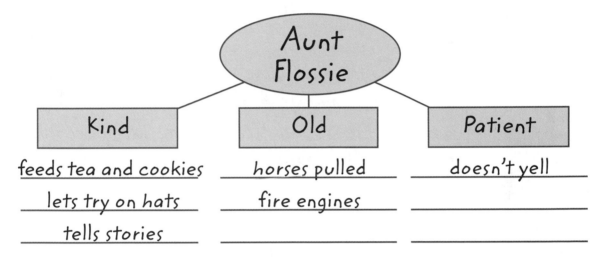

Kind	Old	Patient
feeds tea and cookies	horses pulled	doesn't yell
lets try on hats	fire engines	
tells stories		

Notice how she put *Aunt Flossie* in the middle. In each box, she wrote something that told about the character. Below each box, she put information from the story to support what she had decided.

Lainey used the web to write this response to the story. Each paragraph is about one of the qualities Lainey thought Aunt Flossie had. Notice how Lainey wrote a topic sentence for each paragraph. She used information from the web to support her topic sentence.

Take a Look

I wish I had an aunt like Flossie. She seems very kind. She gives her nieces cookies and tea when they come to visit. She lets them try on her hats. She tells them stories about each hat.

Aunt Flossie must be kind of old. She is a great-great aunt. She remembers when horses pulled fire engines.

I think Aunt Flossie is patient. When the girls try on her very best Sunday hat, she starts to tell the story. The girls keep interrupting. Aunt Flossie doesn't yell at them. She lets them help her tell the story.

Tips for Responding to Fiction

Prewriting Make a Plan

▶ Decide what qualities you think a character has in a fiction story you have read.

▶ Put your ideas on a web.

▶ Look for information in the story to support each idea. Put it on the web.

Drafting Get Your Thoughts on Paper

▶ Use each quality in a separate paragraph.

Revising Be Sure It Makes Sense

▶ **Organization** Do your supporting sentences stay on topic?

▶ **Sentence Fluency** Did you use some long and some short sentences?

Editing/Proofreading Look Closely at the Details

▶ **Conventions** Indent each paragraph.

▶ **Conventions** Make sure you have used capital letters correctly.

▶ **Conventions** Check your response for spelling mistakes.

Publishing Get Ready to Share Your Response to Fiction

▶ **Presentation** Make a clean copy. Does it look like something you would want to read?

▶ **Presentation** Design a cover for your story. Write your response on the front inside flap.

Responding to Nonfiction

A book can be fiction or nonfiction. **Nonfiction** means that the story or information is about a real person, place, or event. The purpose of nonfiction is usually to inform, explain, or persuade. Sometimes the author of nonfiction has a message he or she wants to give to a reader. When you read nonfiction, you need to keep this in mind.

Whenever you read a book, you have thoughts and opinions about it. These come from your response to the

book—what it says or how it says it. When you look through a nonfiction book, you get an idea of whether you are interested in reading it. Whether you know it or not, you are asking yourself these questions: Do I understand the pictures? Are there enough pictures? Do the pictures help me understand the book? Do the headings give me an idea of what the sections will be about? Do the headings sound like something that would interest me? Is the topic important? Is the writer trying to tell me something?

Try It!
What type of nonfiction book would you be interested in reading?

Using a Graphic Organizer

You can understand what you have read better when you write about your reaction. Kylie's teacher asked the class to respond to a nonfiction book. Kylie chose *Hooray for Orchards!* by Bobbie Kalman, Allison Larin, and Nicki Walker. She used this graphic organizer to help her focus as she read.

This book is about

_____

The author wrote this book because

_____

The reasons I think this are

_____

_____

My opinion

_____

I liked/didn't like it because

_____

_____

Here is what Kylie wrote about *Hooray for Orchards!*

    <u>Hooray for Orchards!</u> is all about fruits and orchards. It gives information about kinds of orchards and what orchards need to grow. The pictures are colorful. They helped me understand what I read.

    I think the writers thought orchards are good things. For one thing, they named the book <u>Hooray for Orchards!</u> They also said we should be thankful to orchard growers.

    I agree that orchards are important. I am glad I can get fruit from an orchard. I say hooray for orchards too.

Tips for Responding to Nonfiction

Prewriting Make a Plan
▶ Use a graphic organizer.
▶ Read the book carefully.
▶ Fill in the graphic organizer.

Drafting Get Your Thoughts on Paper
▶ Write your ideas down quickly. Use your graphic organizer.

Revising Be Sure It Makes Sense
▶ **Ideas** Is your response to the book clear?
▶ **Organization** Did you answer each part of the graphic organizer?

Editing/Proofreading Look Closely at the Details
▶ **Conventions** Did you spell everything correctly?
▶ Did you capitalize the title?

Publishing Get Ready to Share Your Response to Nonfiction
▶ **Presentation** Make a clean copy. Could you add a picture to make it more appealing to your reader?
▶ Share your response with a friend who has read the book. Compare responses.

Fun Fact

In the library, nonfiction books have numbers on the spines.

Book Review

When you write a book review, you are telling others what you thought about a book. Reading your review will help them decide if they want to read the book.

Book Review for Fiction

Fiction, stories that are made up, has characters, action, setting, and ideas. For a fiction book, begin by giving the title of the book and the author. Then create a paragraph that gives a short summary. You may want to include **who** the main character is, **what** happened to the character, **when** the story happened, and **where** the story took place. A second paragraph should tell what you thought about the book. You should give reasons for your opinion.

Title: <u>A Chair for My Mother</u>
Author: Vera B. Williams

Summary

Who? a girl, her mom, her grandma
What? saving for a new chair
When? after a fire
Where? a house and an apartment
My Opinion: I liked it. It had a happy ending.

Here is the book report Pilar wrote.

<u>A Chair for My Mother</u> ◀ **Title**
by Vera Williams ◀ **Author**

   A girl lived with her mom
and her grandma in a house.
After the house burned, the girl,
her mom, and grandma moved ◀ **Summary**
into an apartment. They needed
a new chair. The little girl's
mother started saving money for
a comfortable chair. Every day
they counted the money. Finally,
they saved enough and bought a
big chair with pink flowers.
   I liked this book even though
it had a sad part. The chair ◀ **Opinion**
looked comfortable. The girl, her
mom, and her grandma were
all happy to have a new chair.

Tips for Writing a Fiction Book Review

Prewriting Make a Plan

▶ Set up a graphic organizer.

▶ Keep *who, what, when,* and *where* in mind as you read the book.

Drafting Get Your Thoughts on Paper

▶ Quickly get your thoughts down on paper.

▶ Leave spaces for words you can't think of or can't spell.

Revising Be Sure It Makes Sense

▶ **Organization** Did you pick out the most important things in your summary?

▶ **Voice** Did you make your summary sound as though you enjoyed or didn't enjoy the book?

▶ **Sentence Fluency** Did you use sentences of different lengths?

Editing/Proofreading Look Closely at the Details

▶ **Conventions** Are your paragraphs indented?

▶ Is your title underlined? Is it capitalized correctly?

Publishing Get Ready to Share Your Fiction Book Review

▶ **Presentation** Make a clean copy. Is your review easy to read?

▶ Ask your teacher if you can post your book review in your classroom.

Book Review for Nonfiction

Nonfiction means that the story or information is about a real person, place, or event. The purpose of nonfiction is usually to inform, explain, or persuade. Begin with the title of the book and the author. Write a paragraph that tells what the book was about and what you learned from it. Then include a paragraph about what you thought about the book. It is okay if you don't like a book, but you should remember to give good reasons.

Ali used this graphic organizer for the nonfiction book *Germs Make Me Sick!* by Melvin Berger.

Title: *Germs Make Me Sick!*

Author: Melvin Berger

Summary

What was it about?

germs

What did I learn?

everywhere

viruses

bacteria

blood kills germs

My Opinion

didn't like

germs are gross

Here is the book review Ali wrote for his nonfiction book.

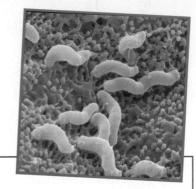

<u>Germs Make Me Sick!</u>
by Melvin Berger

This book was all about germs. I learned that germs are all around us. Some germs are bacteria. Some are viruses. Your blood can kill germs, but not always. When it can't, you get sick.

I learned a lot from this book, but I did not like it. Germs are gross and scary.

Reading Your Writing

When writing a book review, your summary is very important. If you tell your readers too much, they will not need to read the book. If you don't tell them enough, they will not want to read the book.

Tips for Writing a Nonfiction Book Review

Prewriting Make a Plan
▶ Use a graphic organizer that will help you focus as you read the book.
▶ Remember to give reasons for your opinion.

Drafting Get Your Thoughts on Paper
▶ Get your thoughts down quickly.
▶ Write on every other line so you will have room to make changes.

Revising Be Sure It Makes Sense
▶ **Organization** Did you leave anything out? Check your graphic organizer.

Editing/Proofreading Look Closely at the Details
▶ **Conventions** Did you spell the author's name correctly? Did you capitalize each sentence?

Publishing Get Ready to Share Your Nonfiction Book Review
▶ **Presentation** Does your book review look easy to read?
▶ Send your book review to *Stone Soup*, P.O. Box 83, Santa Cruz, CA 95063.
▶ Take your book review to your local library and ask if they will post it on a bulletin board.

Explain a Process

When you tell someone how to do something or how to get somewhere, your purpose is to explain. Giving directions or explaining how to do something takes some practice. You must choose your words and write your sentences carefully. It's very important to keep your audience in mind when you explain something. A first grader will not be able to read the same words as an adult. You will also need to use shorter sentences for a first grader. No matter who your audience is, you must use words they will understand. You must explain step-by-step so your reader will be able to follow along.

Putting Things in Order

When you explain a process, you tell someone how to do something. You might explain how to tie a shoe, wash the dog, or wrap a present. To get started, imagine how to do the task in your mind.

Nick thought about how he planted seeds in his garden last summer. Here are the notes he made as he thought about what he'd had to do.

1. break up the ground
2. make a hole
3. put in the seed
4. cover it
5. water it

Signal Words

When you are explaining a process, signal words such as *first*, *next*, *then*, *after*, *before*, and *finally* can be very useful. These words will help you keep the steps in the right order. They will also help your reader follow the order better.

Here is the paragraph Nick wrote to tell first graders how to plant a seed. Notice how he used signal words.

Take a Look

Let me tell you how to plant a seed. First, break up the ground. Next, make a hole. Poke your finger into the ground up to your first knuckle. Then, put the seed in the hole. Then, cover it with dirt. Finally, water the seed.

Tips for Explaining a Process

Prewriting ▶ Make a Plan

▶ Imagine step-by-step the process you are going to explain.

▶ Write brief notes for each step. You may wish to number them.

Drafting ▶ Get Your Thoughts on Paper

▶ Write your ideas quickly.

▶ Circle any words you cannot spell or think you will change.

Revising ▶ Be Sure It Makes Sense

▶ **Organization** Did you remember all the steps? Are the steps in the correct order?

▶ Ask someone to follow your steps and suggest changes.

Editing/Proofreading ▶ Look Closely at the Details

▶ **Conventions** Did you spell all of the words correctly? Did you use good grammar? Remember, you are telling your audience how to do something.

Publishing ▶ Get Ready to Share Your Explanation of a Process

▶ **Presentation** Make a clean copy of your work. Can you see any parts that look messy?

▶ Draw a diagram to show what you are explaining.

Give Directions

When you give someone directions, you tell the person how to get somewhere. You may use words such as *right*, *left*, and *straight* to clearly explain to your reader. If you are telling someone how to go a long distance, you might also use the word *blocks* or use street names.

To get started, picture a map in your head of the directions you are giving. Imagine you are following the directions yourself. Order is very important. One wrong turn, and your reader is lost!

Nick's mom was coming to help in his classroom. Nick was going to write directions for her. First, he thought about how to get to his room from the front door of the school. This is what he wrote.

turn left
down second hallway
turn right
first hallway

When Nick wrote the directions for his mom, he numbered them. He thought this would make it easier for her to understand.

Take a Look

1. Go through the front door.
2. Turn left.
3. Go to the second hallway.
4. Turn right.
5. Go to the first hallway.
6. Turn left.
7. My room is the first door on the right. It is C6.

Nick was very specific. He told his mom how many hallways, how many doors, and which way to turn whenever there was a choice.

Try It!
Imagine your grandpa is visiting your school for the first time. What directions would you give him to get to the office?

Tips for Giving Directions

Prewriting Make a Plan

▶ Picture in your mind the route someone will take, or walk the route if you can.

▶ Make notes as you go.

▶ Write down helpful information, such as what your reader will see along the way.

Drafting Get Your Thoughts on Paper

▶ Write your directions quickly while you have the route pictured in your mind.

▶ Cross out or circle words you might change later.

Revising Be Sure It Makes Sense

▶ **Organization** Did you remember all the steps? Are they in the correct order?

▶ **Word Choice** Did you use precise direction words for your audience, such as *left, right, north,* or *south?*

Editing/Proofreading Look Closely at the Details

▶ **Conventions** Are your directions given in the present tense? Did you capitalize each sentence?

Publishing Get Ready to Share Your Directions

▶ **Presentation** Make a clean copy of your directions. Are they easy to read?

▶ Draw a map to include with the directions.

News Stories

A **news story** is an accurate report about a person or an event that is happening now. The writer must report a news story in a way that makes the reader care about it. Its purpose is to inform readers. A news story should include only facts, no opinions. Readers count on news stories to be accurate and not take sides. Many people form opinions based on news stories, but if the facts are not accurate, readers cannot make the best decisions. For example, a news story might report on a new toy so that parents can decide if it's safe for their children.

News stories should include information that answers the five Ws.

Who?	Who was involved or whom does it affect?
What?	What did he or she do? What happened?
When?	When did the event take place?
Where?	Where did the event take place?
Why?	Why did the person do what he or she did? Why did the event happen?

Try It!

Think of something that happened at school recently. Answer the five Ws about what happened.

Parts of a News Story

Here are the parts of a news story.

Headline

This is a title for a news story. It is usually short. It gives the reader an idea of what the article is about in a few words.

Byline

This tells who wrote the news story.

Lead

This is the first paragraph. The five Ws are answered in the lead. This is the part that convinces the reader to read more.

Body

This comes after the lead. Details are given in this part. More information about the five Ws is given in the body. Sometimes people are quoted in this part.

Ending

This finishes the news story. It should not include any new information. It should just be a summary of the news story.

How do you get the answers to the five Ws?

1. **Observation** If you were there, you can report what you saw and heard.
2. **Interviews** If you were not there, you can talk to people who were. **Remember:** a news story must be accurate, so stick to the facts. If someone tells you what he or she thinks, make sure that is clear so readers will know it is not a fact.

Alicia Gonzales, age 8, near the end of her jump-a-thon.

Headline ▶ **Evergreen Third Grader Is Grand Champion**

Byline ▶ by Kirk Wade

Lead ▶ Alicia Gonzales, an Evergreen Elementary third grader, is the grand champion rope jumper from Allen County. Alicia jumped for a record two hours and ten minutes at the North Side Mall yesterday. She raised a total of $600 for her community shelter.

Alicia started training a year ago after reading about the great need for food and warm clothing donations during the winter months at the High Hopes Shelter. She got sponsors through her parents' work and family and friends.

"I am grateful to everyone who supported me and donated to this important cause," Alicia said, after catching her breath. "My **◀ Body** parents were very helpful, too. They made sure I ate right and built up my time slowly."

Alicia plans to do this every year, at least until she **◀ Ending** gets to high school. Then she plans to find another way to help support the shelter.

Reading Your Writing

Make sure your facts are correct. Don't include opinions. Your news story should inform your reader. Make sure it answers the five Ws.

Tips for Writing a News Story

Prewriting Make a Plan
- ▶ Do you have the answers for the five Ws?

Drafting Get Your Thoughts on Paper
- ▶ Start with the lead.
- ▶ Write quickly, getting down all the important information.
- ▶ Write a headline that lets your readers know the subject of the news story.

Revising Be Sure It Makes Sense
- ▶ **Organization** Is your story accurate? Did you stick to the facts?
- ▶ Did you cover the five Ws in the lead?
- ▶ **Voice** Did you convince your audience they wanted to read your news story?
- ▶ **Sentence Fluency** Did you tell your news story quickly and simply?

Editing/Proofreading Look Closely at the Details
- ▶ **Conventions** Check your spelling. If you are unsure of a word, look it up in the dictionary. Check capitalization and punctuation.

Publishing Get Ready to Share Your News Story
- ▶ **Presentation** Make a clean copy of your news story so it is easy to read and appealing to your readers. Publish it in your school or classroom newspaper or submit it to your local newspaper for publication.

Research Reports

A good way to share what you know or have learned is through a **research report.** The purpose of a research report is to give information about real facts, ideas, or events and explain what you think they mean. The information can be checked by looking in other sources, such as nonfiction books, magazine articles, encyclopedias, newspapers, or the Internet.

Informational text

▶ provides information
▶ is about real facts, ideas, or events
▶ gets straight to the point
▶ gives events in the order they happened
▶ may be divided into sections by topic, with headings
▶ may have photographs, diagrams, or illustrations with captions
▶ has information that can be checked in other sources

Selecting a Topic

Selecting a topic can take some time. Here is what George did as he tried to decide on a topic:

▶ thought about what he was interested in

▶ thought about things he would like to learn more about

▶ talked to his friends

▶ went to the library to get ideas from books

Finally, George decided to write about animals in his home state. He knew he had to narrow his topic because there were too many animals to be able to write about all of them. He thought he would narrow it down to three. He knew he would have to see what he could find in the library before deciding which three.

Gathering Information

The first thing George did was to find a list of the animals in New Mexico. From that list, he chose to learn more about the prairie dog, the roadrunner, and the horned lizard.

George looked for books and encyclopedia articles on each animal. He read each one carefully.

Try It!

What do you think would make an interesting topic for a research report?

Organizing Information

George wanted to remember what he was reading. He also wanted all the information he gathered to be in one place. He used this graphic organizer to put the information he gathered in order. George read carefully. Then he used his own words to write phrases to help him remember what he wanted to write about.

Animals in New Mexico			◀ Topic

prairie dog	roadrunner	horned lizard	◀ Subtopics
small	20–24 inches	horns above eyes	
hairy	walks or runs	changes color	◀ Facts or details
short legs and tail		hibernates	
bark			

many more	◀ Ending

Here is George's draft. Notice how each subtopic is a separate paragraph.

There are many animals in new mexico. Some live in the dezert. I will tell you about the prairie dog, the road runner, and the horned lizard.

The prarie dog is small. It is very hairy. It has short legs. It has a short tail. They can bark. Some people keep them as pets. I have a pet cat.

The roadrunner is a big bird. It is about 20 to 24 inches long from its beek to its tail. It cannot fly very well. Most of the time it walks or runs. Roadrunners eat rattlesnakes.

The horned lizard is very scary looking. It has horns above its eyes. It can change colors. Horned lizards hibernate.

Here is George's final draft. Notice the changes he made.

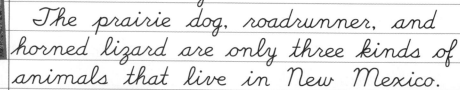

There are many animals in New Mexico. I will tell you about the prairie dog, the roadrunner, and the horned lizard.

The prairie dog is small and very hairy. It has short legs and a short tail.

The roadrunner is a big bird. It is about 20 to 24 inches long from its beak to its tail. It cannot fly very well, so most of the time it walks or runs.

The horned lizard has horns above its eyes. It can change color so it's hard to see. Horned lizards hibernate during the winter.

The prairie dog, roadrunner, and horned lizard are only three kinds of animals that live in New Mexico.

Tips for Writing a Research Report

Prewriting Make a Plan

▶ Choose a topic you know something about or would like to learn more about.

▶ Gather information on the topic.

▶ Put your information in a graphic organizer.

Drafting Get Your Thoughts on Paper

▶ Follow your graphic organizer to write a draft.

Revising Be Sure It Makes Sense

▶ **Ideas** Are your facts correct?

▶ **Organization** Do you have a paragraph that introduces your report and one that ends it?

▶ Are your paragraphs organized by topic? Have you stayed on the topic in each one?

▶ **Sentence Fluency** Did you use some short sentences and some long ones?

Editing/Proofreading Look Closely at the Details

▶ **Conventions** Did you remember to indent each paragraph? Did you spell everything correctly?

Publishing Get Ready to Share Your Research Report

▶ **Presentation** Make a clean copy of your informational report.

▶ Add drawings or photographs if you can.

Narrative Writing

Narrative writing tells a story. The story can be true or make-believe. When you write a story, you are telling your readers what happened. Your story needs a beginning, a middle, and an end. It also needs a setting and characters. Look on the next page for some different kinds of stories you can write.

Personal Narratives

Good writers often write about what they know best. One of the things you know best is yourself. When you write a story about yourself and your own life, it is called a **personal narrative.**

Think about all the things that have happened to you. Look at this list. How many of the things on the list have you done?

▶ learning to ride a bike
▶ going on vacation
▶ wishing for a special gift
▶ playing with friends
▶ moving
▶ celebrating a holiday
▶ playing sports
▶ exploring
▶ participating in a contest

You could write a personal narrative about any one of the items on the list. You should choose something that was important to you. Maybe it was something you thought was exciting or maybe you learned something. If you can remember clearly what you thought about something, it will be easier to write about it.

Try It!
If you had to write about one event in your life, what would it be?

Creating a Graphic Organizer

It is important to help your reader feel involved in your writing. When you describe your feelings, the setting, or the situation well, your reader gets caught up in the story.

Take a Look

Here is a graphic organizer Lee used to plan his personal narrative about the first time he rode in an airplane.

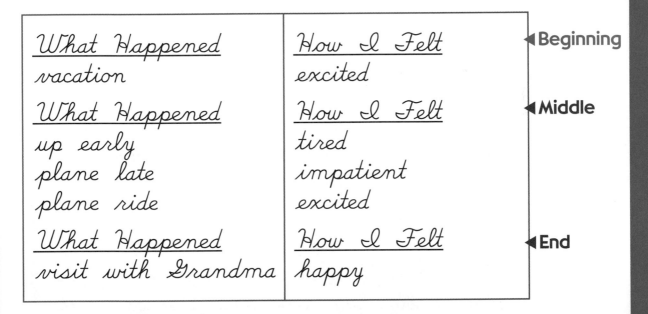

What Happened	How I Felt	
vacation	excited	◀ Beginning
What Happened	How I Felt	
up early	tired	◀ Middle
plane late	impatient	
plane ride	excited	
What Happened	How I Felt	
visit with Grandma	happy	◀ End

The beginning of your personal story must get the reader interested. The middle should tell all about the event. The ending should wrap things up for the reader.

Here is Lee's personal narrative.

> This summer my mom and dad told me we were taking a plane to see Grandma. I had never been on a plane. I was very excited.
>
> We left early in the morning. I was very tired. They told us at the airport our plane was late. I didn't want to wait.
>
> When we got on the plane, I sat next to the window. I saw houses, cars, and even mountains. It was really neat.
>
> Finally we were there. I ran into Grandma's arms and she gave me a big hug. We had a nice visit.

Tips for Writing a Personal Narrative

Prewriting Make a Plan
▶ Think of a meaningful event in your life.
▶ Use a graphic organizer to help organize your thoughts.
▶ Write down what happened and how you felt.

Drafting Get Your Thoughts on Paper
▶ Write your thoughts quickly.
▶ Follow your graphic organizer carefully.

Revising Be Sure It Makes Sense
▶ **Organization** Does your beginning pull the reader in?
▶ **Voice** Can your reader tell what you were feeling?
▶ **Sentence Fluency** Did you use variety in your sentences or did you start them all the same way?

Editing/Proofreading Look Closely at the Details
▶ **Conventions** Did you indent each paragraph?
▶ Do you have any run-on sentences or fragments?

Publishing Get Ready to Share Your Story
▶ **Presentation** Make a clean copy. Does your work look inviting?
▶ Add photographs or illustrations.

Biographies

Writing about the life of a real person is called a **biography.** Anyone can be the subject of a biography. The person may be alive today or have lived in the past. Often, a biography is about the life of a person who has done important things or made a difference, but it doesn't have to be. Any person can be the subject of a biography. All that you need is a person to write about and an audience to read it.

A biography is different from a story because everything and everyone in a biography is true and real. A biography is different than an informational report because a biography is organized in the order things happened in the person's life.

Try It!
Name two people whose biographies you would like to read or write.

What Makes It a Biography?

A biography

▶ is about a real person's life, written by someone else
▶ gives important information about a person's life
▶ tells what the person did, said, and thought
▶ may be about the person's whole life, or just an important part
▶ is often told in the order events happened

What Is in a Biography?

A biography may include

▶ the dates of a person's birth and death
▶ the person's family history
▶ important events in the person's life
▶ quotes from the person

Gathering Information for a Biography

Because a biography is a true story about a real person, you must learn about the person before you can write about him or her. How can you do that?

Interviews

If the person is alive, you may talk to him or her, or others who know that person. You may also talk to someone who used to know the person.

Sample Interview Questions
▶ What are some of your earliest memories?
▶ What was it like growing up in your family?
▶ What advice do you have for students today?

Research

You could look in newspapers, magazines, or encyclopedias or search the Internet at school if the person is famous. Then, take notes on what you read, using your own words. Write down the title of each source you use.

You Would Look For
▶ dates
▶ important events
▶ works or deeds

It takes a lot of time and research to write about a person's entire life. You may want to write about just a short time period or one or two important events in the person's life.

Creating a Time Line

Sofia decided to write about the Brothers Grimm. She reread the article about them that she had read in class. Sofia decided that the best way to organize her information was with a time line.

Date:	1785	1786	1796	1798
Event:	Jacob born	Wilhelm born	their father dies	moved to Cassell to go to school

1812	1859	1863
Nursery and Household Tales published	Wilhelm dies	Jacob dies

Sofia's time line starts with the birth of the brothers. Her time line ends with the death of the brothers. Events on the time line are in the order they happened.

Try It!
What does Sofia's time line tell you about the Brothers Grimm?

Here is Sofia's biography of the Brothers Grimm.

Jacob and Wilhelm Grimm were brothers. Jacob was born in 1785. Wilhelm was born in 1786. They were born in Hanau, Germany.

In 1796, their life changed. Their father died. In 1798 the brothers were sent to Cassell, Germany, to go to school. Later, Jacob and Wilhelm went to Marburg, Germany, to study law. Then they changed their minds. The brothers liked to read and wanted to save the stories, songs, and ballads of Germany.

The brothers started asking people to tell them stories. In 1812 they published Nursery and Household Tales. They also wrote a book about German folktales.

The brothers lived a long life. In 1859 Wilhelm died. Jacob died in 1863. They are buried in Berlin, Germany.

Tips for Writing a Biography

Prewriting Make a Plan
▶ Think of someone you admire and think others will as well.
▶ Interview that person or do research to learn more about him or her.
▶ Take notes on your graphic organizer.

Drafting Get Your Thoughts on Paper
▶ Write your thoughts down quickly.

Revising Be Sure It Makes Sense
▶ **Organization** Are the events in the order in which they happened?
▶ **Word Choice** Did you choose descriptive words to write about the person and their important events?

Editing/Proofreading Look Closely at the Details
▶ **Conventions** Did you spell the name of the person correctly?
▶ Did you use quotations correctly?

Publishing Get Ready to Share Your Story
▶ **Presentation** Make a clean copy in the form of a book.
▶ Add photographs or illustrations.

Fun Fact
The 1999 Caldecott Medal winner, *Snowflake Bentley,* is a biography about a photographer who took pictures of snowflakes.

Realistic Stories

A **realistic story** contains people, places, and events that are made up, but could be real. A story about a boy who wants a puppy for his birthday would be realistic. The boy and the puppy are not real, but they seem real.

When you write a realistic story, you use your imagination to write a story that entertains your audience. Your story can have funny characters, exciting places, or strange events that could be true. That's what makes it different from a fantasy. In fantasy, things happen that could never really happen.

Try It!

Which of the ideas below could you use to write a realistic story?

▶ Two friends try out for a team.
▶ A girl meets a singing turtle by a pond.
▶ Your neighbor's dog wins the spelling bee at school.
▶ A boy gets a brand-new bicycle for his birthday.

Parts of a Realistic Story

A realistic story has a plot, one or more characters, and a setting. The plot of a realistic story has events that could happen in real life. The characters act like real people or animals would. The setting is a place that is real or could be real.

Putting the "Real" in Your Story

The "real" in your story begins with an idea. Details of your ideas make the characters and events come to life.

You can get many ideas for realistic stories from things and places around you. Something at school may give you an idea. An event in your neighborhood or town can get you started.

The idea for the student model on the next page came from an event at Josh's school. Every year his school has a Games Day. Josh decided to use this event for his story. Although he made up the story, he wanted it to seem real. Josh added details to make his character, Nate, seem real. He made Nate nervous before the race. He also made Nate dream of winning a blue ribbon. With his idea and details, Josh made Nate seem like a real person. You can do the same thing in your stories.

Try It!
▶ While you're reading Josh's story, ask yourself if the characters, setting, and events are realistic.
▶ Pay attention to the details in Josh's story that make it realistic.

Here is a realistic story that was written by Josh.

Nate got to school early on Friday morning. He was excited about Games Day. Nate saw his friend Brad on the playground.

"Are you nervous?" asked Brad.

"A little," said Nate.

Nate was one of the fastest runners in third grade. Today he might win a blue ribbon. He had a dream about winning a blue ribbon.

It was time for the race. The runners lined up. At the signal, they all started to run.

Nate got a good start, but Tina was ahead of him. He thought about the ribbon. He ran faster and faster. He passed Tina and crossed the finish line. He won!

Later, Nate walked home. He looked at his blue ribbon. He smiled and thought, "I guess dreams do come true, sometimes."

Tips for Writing a Realistic Story

Prewriting Make a Plan

▶ List some things you have done.

▶ List some places you have been or would like to visit.

▶ List some interesting people you have known.

▶ Choose a setting, some events for your plot, and the characters for your story.

Drafting Get Your Thoughts on Paper

▶ Write your realistic story. Use your notes.

▶ Don't worry about mistakes. You can correct them later.

Revising Be Sure It Makes Sense

▶ **Ideas** Could your setting be a real place?

▶ Do your characters act real? If they don't, change how they act and what they say.

▶ **Sentence Fluency** Are your sentences smooth and easy to read?

Editing/Proofreading Look Closely at the Details

▶ **Conventions** Proofread for spelling mistakes.

▶ If you have written dialogue, make sure the punctuation is correct.

Publishing Get Ready to Share Your Realistic Story

▶ **Presentation** Make a neatly typed or written final copy.

Fun Fact

Ramona Quimby is a realistic character created by Beverly Cleary, who wrote many funny books about Ramona and her adventures.

Mysteries

A **mystery** occurs when something happens and how or why it happened is not clear. The person who solves the mystery is called a detective. Two famous fictional detectives are Sherlock Holmes and Nancy Drew.

Imagine this: Fred left his library book on the kitchen table. When he went to get it an hour later, it was gone. Where could it be? Now you have a mystery.

To write a mystery, you can begin with a problem. Perhaps something is missing. Maybe something has been damaged, or something has appeared. Then you give clues so your readers can solve the mystery. Sometimes there are clues that do not help. These are given to throw the reader off track. They make the reader think about other solutions for the mystery.

Take a Look

Below are some possible solutions to the mystery of Fred's missing library book.

Mom left the house about half an hour ago. Maybe she took the book back to the library.

The dog ran off with it. He is curious and always takes things off the table.

Fred left it somewhere else. He is very forgetful.

Try It!
Think of another possible solution to the mystery of Fred's missing library book.

Parts of a Mystery

Like other stories, a mystery has characters, a setting, and a problem in the plot. The plot must have a crime or mysterious happening. One of the characters has to solve the mystery. Clues are also part of the plot in a mystery. Clues are hints that might help you solve the mystery. The clues do not tell you the answer.

Suspense and Surprise

You can use suspense and surprise in your mystery. They keep your readers on the edge of their seats. **Suspense** is when your reader isn't sure what will happen next. **Surprise** is when something sudden or unexpected happens.

Here's an example of suspense.

Where could Fred's book be? He couldn't afford to pay for the missing book. What will he do?

This is an example of surprise.

When Fred opened the closet door, hundreds of books fell to the floor.

Here is the beginning of Fred's mystery.

Fred was always reading. He walked around all day with a book in his hands. One day Fred left a library book on the kitchen table. When Fred went back to get the book, it was gone.

Where could the book be? He couldn't afford to pay for the missing book. What will he do?

Fred looked all over for the book. Then he noticed his bookmark on the floor near the rocking chair. Fred went over to investigate. Yes, it was his bookmark all right.

Fred yelled for his sister. "Rita, have you seen my book?"

"Was it the one about planes?"

"Yes. Have you seen it?" Fred said.

"Nope, haven't seen it," Rita answered, a little too quickly.

Tips for Writing a Mystery

Fun Fact

Nate the Great, Cam Jansen, the Boxcar Children, and Encyclopedia Brown are kids who solve mysteries. Check them out the next time you're at the library.

Prewriting ▸ Make a Plan

▶ Think of a problem and several possible solutions.

▶ Plan clues that lead to one of the solutions.

▶ Use a graphic organizer to plan characters, setting, a problem, clues, and a solution.

Drafting ▸ Get Your Thoughts on Paper

▶ Write your mystery.

▶ Follow your graphic organizer.

Revising ▸ Be Sure It Makes Sense

▶ **Word Choice** Do your words add suspense to the mystery?

▶ **Voice** Does the personality of your detective come through?

▶ **Organization** Do your clues add up? Do they lead to a solution?

Editing/Proofreading ▸ Look Closely at the Details

▶ **Conventions** Have you indented each paragraph?

▶ If you used dialogue, have you punctuated it correctly?

Publishing ▸ Get Ready to Share Your Mystery

▶ **Presentation** Make sure your mystery looks neat and is easy to read.

Fantasies

A **fantasy** is a story that has characters, places, or events that could not exist in the real world. Maybe the characters act in a way that is impossible. Is it possible for a carpet to fly? Is it possible for animals to talk or for rain to turn to meatballs? Is there such a place as the Land of Toys? Are elves, unicorns, and hobbits real? All of these things are possible in a fantasy story.

A fantasy story is different from a realistic story. In a realistic story, the characters, setting, and events in the plot could be real but are not. In a fantasy, there might be some things that seem real, but there will be many other things that couldn't be real.

Try It!
Think about the books you have read or the stories you have heard. Which ones were fantasies?

Lee had to write a fantasy story for homework. He looked around his room to get ideas. Here is the first part of Lee's fantasy story.

One morning, on a very gray day, Oswald woke up feeling kind of strange. He stretched his fins, yawned, and looked around. Across the room, he saw his fish tank. His boy was in it! Sleeping! The boy who always came to feed him, change his water, and talk to him was in his tank. Sleeping!

Oswald got up to get a closer look and was surprised to find out that he could actually walk. His fins were moving just like feet. He walked across the room to his fish tank. He looked in. Just then his boy yawned, stretched, and woke up.

What's So Special About Fantasy?

Look carefully at the chart below. It shows what might be in a fantasy. When you write a fantasy, you may wish to include one or more of these things. You do not have to include all of them.

What is in a fantasy

people, animals, and things that have powers they don't have in the real world

events that could not happen in the real world

places that do not exist

creatures that do not exist

Examples

disappearing people, talking elephants, flying cars

a rainbow in the dark, boats sailing on clouds

a place where you never grow old

unicorns, elves

Try It!

Look back at Lee's fantasy to answer this question.

Which events were not possible?

Tips for Writing a Fantasy

Prewriting **Make a Plan**

▶ Look for a story in your portfolio that you could make into a fantasy.

▶ Think of which element or elements of fantasy you want to include. Think about how you will include them.

Drafting **Get Your Thoughts on Paper**

▶ Write on every other line so you will have space to make changes later.

Revising **Be Sure It Makes Sense**

▶ **Organization** Do you have a good beginning, middle, and end?

▶ **Sentence Fluency** Have you used some long and some short sentences?

Editing/Proofreading **Look Closely at the Details**

▶ **Conventions** Proofread for spelling.

▶ Have you capitalized proper nouns?

Publishing **Get Ready to Share Your Fantasy**

▶ **Presentation** Make a clean copy and illustrate it.

▶ Consider putting it in your portfolio to make into a puppet show or play.

► Tall Tales

A **tall tale** is a made-up story that usually exaggerates or stretches the truth. It includes unlikely events or problems and creative solutions. The main character usually isn't real. Tall tales are often funny and usually larger than life. A tall tale is different from a realistic story. Not everything in a tall tale could be real.

Have you ever read a story about Paul Bunyan, John Henry, Pecos Bill, or Shorty Long? They are all characters in tall tales.

Take a Look

Here is an excerpt from *John Henry* by Julius Lester. This is the night that John Henry was born. Notice the exaggeration.

He grew and he grew and he grew. He grew until his head and shoulders busted through the roof which was over the porch. John Henry thought that was the funniest thing in the world. He laughed so loud, the sun got scared. It scurried from behind the moon's skirts and went to bed, which is where it should've been all the while.

Try It!
Think of an exaggeration for one of the following situations.
▶ what happened to your homework
▶ what will happen if you eat peas
▶ a fish you saw over the weekend

Parts of a Tall Tale

Like a realistic story, a tall tale has one or more characters, a setting, and events in a plot. In some tall tales, characters, settings, and events might seem as if they could be real, but there is something about them that is hard to believe. Other tall tales are not believable at all, such as the sun crying or a wolf singing.

When you are planning what you will write about, think about exaggeration, unlikely situations or problems, and creative solutions. Think of situations you have been in, things you have read about, or people you have known. Then, try to exaggerate them. Talk to your friends and write down any ideas they have for characters, unlikely events, or solutions.

Here is a tall tale that Keisha wrote after reading several tall tales on her own.

Amelia was a character. No one knows where she came from or how old she was. What people do know is that Amelia was the fastest and strongest person around. She was so quick she could run faster than lightning. She was so strong, she could pick up a horse with one hand.

She wasn't just fast and strong. It seemed like Amelia was always helping people out, without even being asked. One day, the people of Big Gulch, Oklahoma, needed help in a big way. A telegram had come saying that a runaway train was going to hit Big Gulch General Store.

It didn't take Amelia long to figure out what to do. She went out of town to where the train tracks ran near a cotton field. She pulled up the tracks and headed them into the field.

That train came along and followed those tracks right into the field. It slowed down in the soft cotton and finally stopped. Not one person got hurt, thanks to Amelia's quick thinking. Everybody was so thankful, they made Amelia the sheriff of Big Gulch.

Getting Started

Writing a tall tale isn't easy. It took Keisha a long time to do her prewriting. She had to think hard about what she wanted Amelia to be faster than. She thought of all kinds of fast things before she decided on lightning.

Keisha has made a good start. She can put her tall tale in her portfolio and add to it later.

What Makes a Tall Tale a Tall Tale

Here are definitions for the parts of a tall tale and examples of how those parts were used in the book *John Henry* by Julius Lester.

Exaggeration

Something is made out to be bigger or more than it is.

Example: John Henry grew so big the day he was born that his head went through the porch roof.

Unlikely Event or Problem

An event or problem that couldn't really happen.

Examples

Event: A rainbow wrapped itself around John Henry's shoulders.

Problem: A huge boulder in the road could not be broken with dynamite.

Creative Solution to a Problem

A good way of solving a problem that couldn't really be done.

Example: When a boulder couldn't be broken up by dynamite, John Henry broke it up with his two sledge hammers and finished building a road at the same time.

Tips for Writing a Tall Tale

Prewriting Make a Plan

▶ Look through your portfolio for ideas.

▶ Talk to your friends.

▶ Make notes on characters, setting, problem, and solution. Use a graphic organizer.

Drafting Get Your Thoughts on Paper

▶ Put your notes into sentences quickly.

▶ Circle any words you might want to change later.

Revising Be Sure It Makes Sense

▶ **Voice** Does it sound as though you enjoy the characters and events you are telling about?

▶ **Word Choice** Are your words helping your readers imagine the character, setting, and events?

Editing/Proofreading Look Closely at the Details

▶ **Conventions** Make sure your verb tense is the same throughout your tall tale.

▶ Capitalize proper nouns and the names of special places, such as rivers and mountains.

Publishing Get Ready to Share Your Tall Tale

▶ **Presentation** Make a clean copy in the form of a tall book.

▶ Put your tall tale in your portfolio so you can add more later.

Fun Fact

Some people say John Henry was a real person who helped build a railroad tunnel in West Virginia between 1870 and 1873.

A **play** is a story that is written to be performed in front of an audience. The writer of the play tells the story by writing what the characters do and say.

Like a story, a play has characters, a setting, and events in the plot. The characters are the actors in the play. They may be people or animals. The setting in a play is also called the scene. It is where the action takes place and when it takes place. When you tell where and when the story takes place, you are setting the scene.

A play is different from a story or report. Stories and reports are written to be read. A play is written to be performed. A play has stage directions, lines, and props. Stories and reports don't have them.

Try It!

Imagine you are writing a play about your classroom. Name three characters. Set the scene.

Parts of a Play

Imagine this play: It is the first day of school. The teacher is Mr. Dawes. The students are talking and laughing when the bell rings. The examples that follow each definition below are based on this play.

Stage Directions

These are the directions that tell the characters where to move or how to speak. These are given in parentheses so the performers know it is something to do, not say. They are often in italics. You can do this if you write your play on a computer at school.

Example: (The bell rings and the students go to their seats.)

Lines

These are the words spoken by the characters. The speaker's name is at the beginning of the first line. It is written with all capital letters and followed by a colon.

Example:
MR. DAWES: Good morning, class. I am your new teacher, Mr. Dawes.

Props

Props are objects that will be used by the actors and sounds that are made offstage. These are part of the stage directions.

Example: a bell ringing, desks and chairs for Dawes and students

Kay's play is based on the story of the three little pigs. First, Kay listed the characters and the important events in the order they happened. Then, she wrote the dialogue for each character. Finally, she went back and filled in stage directions.

Here is the beginning of Kay's play.

Characters: Pig #1
             Pig #2
             Pig #3
             Big, Bad Wolf

Time: a long time ago

Place: in the country, outside

Pig #1: I think it is time for me to build my own house. I can't afford much. I guess I'll use straw.

Pig #2: (watching) That will never work. It won't be sturdy enough.

Pig #1: What do you know? You don't even have a house.

(Just as Pig #1 finishes the house, the Wolf enters from the left, whistling. He huffs, and puffs, and blows the house down. Pig #1 runs across the stage, squealing.)

(Pig #2 is building a house of sticks. Pig #1 runs up to him. Pig #2 doesn't seem to notice that Pig #1 is out of breath.)

Pig #1: Well, you were right about my house. A big, bad wolf came along and blew it down. Can I live with you?

Pig #2: I hate to say I told you so, but I did. You can stay for a while.

(The pigs finish building the house and go inside. The wolf enters and speaks to the audience.)

Wolf: Watch this, I'll get two for the price of one. (He looks toward the house of sticks, cups his hands around his mouth, and yells.) Oh, little pig, could I borrow a couple of apples? I'd like to make a pie. I'll share it.

Pig #2: (bravely) Go away! I don't have any apples.

Wolf: That's not very nice. Let's try this again. Let me in (getting angry) or I'll huff, and I'll puff, and I'll blow your house down!

What Makes a Play a Play

Writing a play takes planning and attention to details. A writer has to decide what characters will say and how they will move on the stage. These details are written as stage directions and dialogue.

What the characters say and the way they say it lets the audience know what each character is like. For example, the wolf starts to sound angry. He doesn't have much patience, and he isn't very nice.

How the characters move also helps us understand them. After the wolf blew down Pig #1's house, the pig ran away squealing. We know that he was afraid.

Try It!
Look back at Kay's play.
▶ Count how many times Pig #1 speaks.
▶ Read the stage directions aloud.
▶ What props will Kay need for this play?

Reading Your Writing
Keep in mind when you write your play that it will be acted out. Your dialogue and stage directions need to make the play come alive.

Tips for Writing a Play

Prewriting Make a Plan
▶ Choose a story you already know.
▶ Develop your stage directions and dialogue based on what will happen in your play.

Drafting Get Your Thoughts on Paper
▶ Write what each character in your play will say.
▶ Add stage directions.

Revising Be Sure It Makes Sense
▶ **Organization** Do your stage directions go with the action that is taking place?
▶ **Ideas** Did you include the most important events from the story you used?

Editing/Proofreading Look Closely at the Details
▶ **Conventions** Did you remember to put the characters' names at the beginning of their lines?
▶ Did you put parentheses around the stage directions?

Publishing Get Ready to Share Your Play
▶ **Presentation** Make a neat copy of your play. Make a cover with the name of the play on it.
▶ Practice and perform your play. Use real people and costumes or puppets.

Descriptive Writing

Descriptive writing gives a clear picture to your readers. It helps your readers see what you see. It helps them hear what you hear. It helps them feel what you feel. The following lesson will give you tips on writing good descriptions.

Writing a Description

A **description** gives details about a person, place, thing, or action. Descriptions create pictures in the minds of readers by telling what you see, hear, feel, smell, or taste. Good descriptions make your writing clearer and more interesting.

Take a Look

Read this descriptive writing from Patricia MacLachlan's story, "Through Grandpa's Eyes." The grandpa in this story is blind.

> *"And somewhere behind the blackbird," he says, listening, "a song sparrow."*
>
> *I hear a scratchy song, and I look and look until I see the earth-colored bird that Grandpa knows is here.*
>
> *Nana calls from the front porch of the house.*
>
> *"Nana's made hot bread for lunch," he tells me happily. "And spice tea." Spice tea is his favorite.*
>
> *I close my eyes, but all I can smell is the wet earth by the river.*

Using Senses in a Description

Knowing how to write a good description will help your reader imagine what you are writing about. Using just the right descriptive words gives your reader a clearer picture of what you are describing. Take a look at this description written by a student.

Take a Look

Haley found a surprise on the table when she came home from school. She decided to write a description about it.

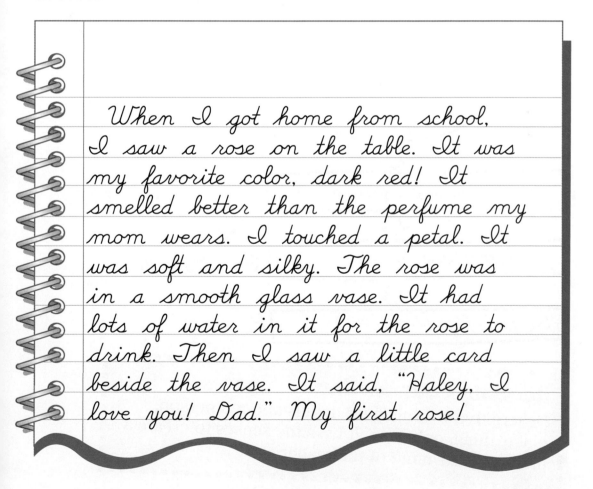

> When I got home from school, I saw a rose on the table. It was my favorite color, dark red! It smelled better than the perfume my mom wears. I touched a petal. It was soft and silky. The rose was in a smooth glass vase. It had lots of water in it for the rose to drink. Then I saw a little card beside the vase. It said, "Haley, I love you! Dad." My first rose!

Organizing a Description

A good **description** uses many senses to describe something. Tell your reader how things look, sound, feel, taste, and smell. You give readers great pictures in their minds when you use several senses to describe things.

A good description is organized. Good organization helps hold your reader's attention. A *top-to-bottom* graphic organizer is one way to organize the details of a description.

Look again at Haley's description. She used a *top-to-bottom* graphic organizer to put the details in order. What details did she put at the top of her organizer? What details did she use in the middle? Finally, what details were at the bottom?

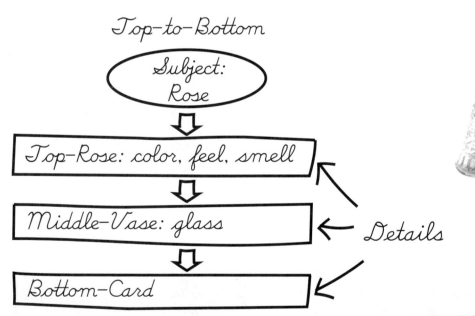

Top-to-Bottom

Subject: Rose

Top-Rose: color, feel, smell

Middle-Vase: glass

Bottom-Card

Details

Tips for Writing a Description

Prewriting **Make a Plan**
- ▶ Read your journal to get ideas of what to write.
- ▶ Use a top-to-bottom graphic organizer to get your details in order.

Drafting **Get Your Thoughts on Paper**
- ▶ Write your description using your graphic organizer.

Revising **Be Sure It Makes Sense**
- ▶ **Sentence Fluency** Make sure you don't start all your sentences the same way.
- ▶ **Word Choice** Do your descriptive words create a picture in your reader's mind?

Editing/Proofreading **Look Closely at the Details**
- ▶ **Conventions** Be sure to put commas in lists of three or more adjectives.
- ▶ Use a dictionary if you are not sure of the spellings of your descriptive words.

Publishing **Get Ready to Share Your Description**
- ▶ **Presentation** Make a neat final copy of your description. Check for eraser marks.

Persuasive Writing

Persuasive writing does two things. It can make readers think or feel a certain way. It can also make readers do something. Sometimes persuasive writing can do both of these things at the same time. Advertisements are one kind of persuasive writing. You will learn about other kinds in the following lessons.

Persuasive Writing

Persuasive writing tries to get a reader to think, feel, or act a certain way. You can help change readers' minds or persuade them to think about or to do something by what you write.

The beginning should catch the reader's attention, tell what the subject is, and how the writer feels about it.

The ending should sum up the reasons given and suggest that the readers take action or accept the writer's opinion.

You have seen ads on television or in magazines. Do the ads make you want the things they're advertising? Here are three traits of good persuasive writing:

1. The reasons given for thinking, feeling, or acting a certain way make good sense.
2. The subject is interesting to your audience.
3. The writing is organized and easy to follow.

Try It!

Which of these sentences is persuasive?

▶ My dad helps me build things with scraps of wood.
▶ If we were served a snack at school, our brains would have the energy they need to help us learn.
▶ There are wild geese at the pond in the city park.

Two Ways to Persuade

There are two methods you can use to persuade readers to think or feel a certain way. You can give facts and good reasons for your idea. You can also tell your readers how you feel about your subject.

Think about your readers. Will they be interested in the same things you are?

Take a Look

Here are two different ways to persuade.

▶ **Facts/Reasons:** Schools should serve a snack at morning recess because some kids don't eat a good breakfast. If kids feel better, they can learn more.

▶ **Feelings:** Schools should serve a snack at morning recess because kids would feel better and be happier and more able to learn if they weren't hungry.

Try It!

Match the subjects for persuasive writing with the readers who will be interested.

3rd Graders   Adults   Both Groups

▶ Everybody deserves to have their newspapers delivered every day.

▶ If recess were 15 minutes longer, kids would be healthier from the exercise.

▶ A day at the zoo can be fun for young and old alike.

Persuasive Paragraphs

Many persuasive paragraphs have three parts: the *topic sentence*, *body*, and *closing sentence*.

1. The *topic sentence* tells the reader what the subject of the paragraph is. It also tells the writer's thoughts or feelings—this is called the "writer's viewpoint"—about the subject.

2. The *body* of a persuasive paragraph gives the reasons and facts to support the writer's viewpoint. The most important reason is often given last.

3. The *closing sentence* sums up the reasons. It also suggests that readers take action or accept the writer's viewpoint about the subject.

Writing the Parts of Persuasive Paragraphs

Choose a topic that you feel strongly about. Ask yourself, "Why is this important to me?" Think about your readers. Will this topic be important to them, too?

What do you want your readers to think or do about the topic? Decide if you will use reasons or feelings to persuade them in the body of your paragraph.

Be sure to mention your best reason or strongest feeling in your closing sentence. Also, tell what action you want your readers to take.

Organizing Persuasive Paragraphs

A good persuasive paragraph makes it easy for readers to follow what you are trying to tell them. Making a web for your topic and reasons is a good way to start organizing your writing.

Jasmine wanted to write about the value of playing board games in class. Here is the web she made.

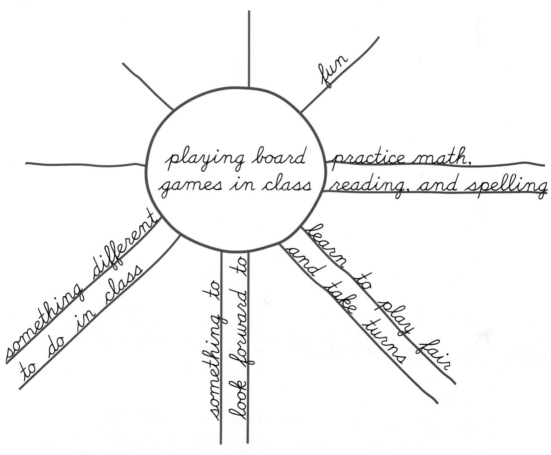

After finishing your web, decide what the most important reason is. Jasmine decided that "practice math, reading, and spelling" was the most important reason in her web. When you are writing the body of the paragraph, you should save that reason for last.

Jasmine thought about who would be interested in board games in class. She thought that kids and teachers would be, and maybe parents and the principal, too.

Jasmine was sure that if people read her paragraph and agreed with her, there could be board games in class. She decided to try to get her persuasive paragraph published in the school newspaper.

Franklin School Kids' Rap

**Have Fun Studying—
Play Games!**

I think that we should be able to play board games in class. By playing games, we would learn to play fair and take turns. We would also get a lot of practice with math, reading, and spelling. There should be board games in class so we can have fun while we are learning.

Try It!

What is the viewpoint in the topic sentence above? How many reasons does Jasmine give in the body of her paragraph? What reasons does she "sum up" in her closing sentence?

Tips for Writing Persuasive Paragraphs

Prewriting Make a Plan

▶ Pick a topic you have strong feelings about. Reading in your journal may give you ideas.

▶ Make a web to organize your topic.

Drafting Get Your Thoughts on Paper

▶ Use your web to help you remember your reasons.

Revising Be Sure It Makes Sense

▶ **Organization** Make sure the topic sentence comes first, the body with the facts, reasons, or feelings is in the middle, and a closing sentence ends your paragraph.

Editing/Proofreading Look Closely at the Details

▶ **Conventions** Correct any spelling mistakes.

▶ Does every sentence have an end mark?

Publishing Get Ready to Share Your Paragraph

▶ **Presentation** Write or type a neat final copy.

▶ Put your paragraph in a school newspaper to persuade others.

Cereal Box Designs

Have you ever taken a good long look at a cereal box? Somebody spent a lot of time and effort designing a cereal box. Why? So you will want that box of cereal. Persuasive writing is not just for the classroom; it's on cereal boxes too!

Ways to Persuade People to Buy

Giving good reasons and facts is one way to get people to buy something. Putting reasons into short phrases that stick in the mind helps people remember them. Describing a thing as the best is another way to persuade people to buy.

Take a Look

Here is a cereal box designed for people who like healthful foods. It uses reasons and facts to persuade people to try this new "good for you" cereal.

NEW!

Packed with Protein Power!

POWER HOUSE
CEREAL

10 grams of **protein** in every serving
Power Bits of **5** Different Toasted **Whole Grains**!
Iron-Rich Raisins and **Protein**-Rich Sunflower Seeds

Another Look at Cereal Box Designs

Here is a cereal box designed for people who like to eat food that looks fun and tastes good. It uses descriptions to persuade people to try this new "fun" cereal.

Try It!
Read the two cereal boxes. Which cereal would you choose? Name three reasons that made you want that cereal.

Poetry

Poetry is very different from other kinds of writing. Think of some poems you have read. They look very different from stories or articles. There is something else about poetry. It can describe things in a way that you may never have thought about before. The lessons on the following pages will give you a chance to write some different kinds of poetry.

Rhyming Poetry

In **poetry** the sound and meaning of words are combined to create images and feelings. Unlike other kinds of writing, poetry is written in lines instead of paragraphs and doesn't always use complete sentences or punctuation. Some poetry rhymes. Three kinds of **rhyming poetry** are the *couplet, triplet,* and *quatrain.*

Take a Look

Couplet: Two lines of rhyming poetry.

> Crash goes the trash can! Clatter and clacket!
> What in the world can be making that racket?
>   –from "Raccoon" by Mary Ann Hoberman

Triplet: Three lines of rhyming poetry. Rhymes can end every line.

> Their daily lives are bland,
> and if they land—
> they're canned.
>   –from "Sardines" by Jack Prelutsky

Quatrain: Four lines of rhyming poetry.

> One day a funny kind of man
> Came walking down the street.
> He wore a shoe upon his head,
> And hats upon his feet.
>   –from "A Funny Man" by Natalie Joan

Reading Your Writing

Poetry is a way for you to share your feelings with your reader. Three rhyming poems are the couplet, the triplet, and the quatrain.

Tips for Writing a Rhyming Poem

Prewriting Make a Plan

▶ Read a lot of rhyming poems before you begin.
▶ Pick a subject that is important or funny to you.
▶ List rhyming words to end your lines.
▶ Choose a type of poem: couplet, triplet, or quatrain.

Drafting Get Your Thoughts on Paper

▶ Write your poem. Use your list of rhyming words.

Revising Be Sure It Makes Sense

▶ **Organization** Do your lines end with rhyming words?
▶ **Sentence Fluency** Lines don't have to be complete sentences, but they do need to sound smooth.

Editing/Proofreading Look Closely at the Details

▶ **Conventions** Correct any spelling mistakes.

Publishing Get Ready to Share Your Poem

▶ **Presentation** Make a neat final copy of your poem. You may want to draw a picture to go with it.
▶ Read it aloud to get ready to share it.

Nonrhyming Poetry

Nonrhyming poetry doesn't have rhyming patterns, but it may have other kinds of patterns. For example, *cinquain poems* always have the same kinds of words and number of words. *Free verse* has no patterns at all.

Take a Look

Cinquain: A poem that is five lines long and follows this special pattern.

Type of Word	Number of words	
Title	one	"Phone"
Description	two	Quiet, sudden
Action	three	Jingling, jangling, wrangling
Feeling or Effect	four	Demanding I pay attention
Synonym for Title	one	TELEPHONE!!!

Free Verse: A poem that can be long or short. It can have some rhyming words but doesn't have to. Here is a free-verse Crow Indian poem.

"The Sun Is a Yellow-Tipped Porcupine . . ."
The sun is a yellow-tipped porcupine
Lolloping through the sky,
Nibbling treetops and grasses and weeds,
Floating on rivers and ponds,
Casting shining barbed quills at the Earth.

Tips for Writing Free Verse

Prewriting Make a Plan

▶ Make a web with your subject in the middle. Put feelings and thoughts about your subject all around.

Drafting Get Your Thoughts on Paper

▶ Write your poem using your web to remember things you want to say.

Revising Be Sure It Makes Sense

▶ **Organization** Read your poem out loud. Every time you pause, begin a new line.

Editing/Proofreading Look Closely at the Details

▶ **Conventions** Make sure your punctuation marks are helping you say what you want.

Publishing Get Ready to Share Your Free-Verse Poem

▶ **Presentation** Decide how you want the lines of your free verse to look on the page.

▶ Make a neat final copy.

Pattern Poetry

Some poetry follows rhyming **patterns.** Other poems follow patterns for length of lines. Some poems follow both patterns.

Some poems use the patterns from a familiar poem or song. The words are different, but the rhyme and length of line patterns are the same.

Take a Look

Do you know the song "I've Been Working on the Railroad"? The poem below uses the same rhyme and line-length patterns.

> "We've Been Working on the Tree House"
> We've been working on the tree house,
> All the weekend long,
> We've been sweating and been hammering,
> And still it looks all wrong.
> Dad, please, please, you have to help us,
> Then the job should go fast;
> We'll wash the car for you, we promise!
> And the tree house will be done at last.

Try It!

Match the familiar song lines to the lines with the same pattern of syllables.

"Happy Birthday to You"

"Yankee Doodle Went to Town"

Will you trade lunch with me

Ever wonder what dogs think

Checklist

▶ Choose a song or poem you know well.

▶ Count the syllables in each line.

▶ List rhyming words that fit your subject.

▶ Sing your song or say your poem out loud as you write. This will help you choose the best words.

Reading Your Writing

Poetry is a way for you to share your feelings with your reader. Some poems can be patterned on other familiar poems or songs.

Fun Fact

What is the most familiar song in the English language? "Happy Birthday to You" is the song sung most often. It was written in 1893 by Mildred Hill and Patty Smith Hill.

Structures of Writing

Words, sentences, and paragraphs are the building blocks of writing. Writers use words to build sentences. They use sentences to build paragraphs. You are a writer. You can do it, too.

What Is a Sentence?

A **sentence** has two parts, a **subject** and a **predicate.** The subject names the person or thing the sentence is about. The predicate tells what the subject is or does. The predicate may be a verb only or a verb plus other words. A sentence always begins with a capital letter and ends with a punctuation mark.

Take a Look

Jenny played a game.

The subject is *Jenny.* It tells what the sentence is about. The predicate is *played a game.* It tells what Jenny did.

Elijah is happy.

This sentence is about Elijah. The subject is *Elijah.* The predicate is *is happy.* It tells what Elijah is.

Try It!

Find the subject and predicate in this sentence:
  My friends eat pizza.

Problems to Avoid in Your Sentences

1. **Fragment:** A group of words that is missing a subject, a predicate, or both.
2. **Run-on:** Two or more sentences that are put together without a conjunction, such as *and* or *but*.
3. **Rambling:** A sentence that has a lot of conjunctions. The conjunctions join sentences that should be written separately.

Take a Look

Fragment: *Ran fast.*
Sentence: *Marcus ran fast.*

Run-on: *My sister's name is Ramona she's a pest.*
Better: *My sister's name is Ramona, and she's a pest.*

Rambling: *My brothers and I went camping and hiked in the woods and swam in the lake and slept in a tent.*
Better: *My brothers and I went camping. We hiked in the woods and swam in the lake. Later, we slept in a tent.*

Try It!
How could you fix this run-on sentence?
I like the weekend my favorite day is Saturday.

Writing Sentences

Good sentences can be short or long, but you shouldn't use too many short sentences together. When writers use a lot of short sentences, they usually repeat words. Combining sentences and taking out the extra words will make your writing easier to read.

Take a Look

Leo likes fish.

He likes broccoli.

He likes milk.

The sentences are short and many words are repeated. You can get rid of the extra words by combining the sentences like this:

Leo likes fish, broccoli, and milk.

The longer sentence has the same meaning as the three short sentences but reads more smoothly.

Other parts of a sentence can be combined also.

Sam looks for crickets every day. Sam feeds his frog every day.
Better: Sam looks for crickets to feed his frog every day.

Bullfrogs can be found in Ohio. Rattlesnakes can be found in Ohio. Bats can be found in Ohio.
Better: Bullfrogs, rattlesnakes, and bats can be found in Ohio.

Trudy's class looked for toads in the garden. They looked for toads near the pond. They looked for toads under a bucket.
Better: Trudy's class looked for toads in the garden, near the pond, and under a bucket.

Try It!

Combine these sentences into one sentence that reads more smoothly.

Oranges have rough skin.

They have bumpy skin.

They have thick skin.

Compound Sentences

Sentences can also be combined without dropping any words. Use all of the words from both sentences, and put them together with *and, but,* or *or.* When you combine two whole sentences, you form a **compound sentence.**

To find out more about using the conjunctions *and, but,* or *or,* see pages 212 and 255.

Take a Look

> *Miriam likes to play soccer and basketball. She does not like to play football.*

These sentences are combined below as a compound sentence.

> *Miriam likes to play soccer and basketball, but she does not like to play football.*

Try It!
Combine these sentences using *but.*
  Frogs have smooth skin. Toads have bumpy skin.

Reading Your Writing
Combine sentences or parts of sentences that will make your writing better and easier to read.

Kinds of Sentences

The four kinds of sentences are **declarative, interrogative, imperative,** and **exclamatory.** Sentences that tell something are statements, or declarative sentences. They end with a period. Sentences that ask something are questions, or interrogative sentences. They end in a question mark. Sentences that tell someone to do something are commands, or imperative sentences. They end with a period. Sentences that show strong feeling are exclamations, or exclamatory sentences. They end with an exclamation point.

Take a Look

Declarative: Jennifer likes to draw pictures.
Interrogative: What does Jennifer like to draw?
Imperative: Look at this picture.
Exclamatory: I love to draw!

Try It!
Change this interrogative sentence so that it is an imperative sentence.
Will you sit in this chair?

Reading Your Writing
Different kinds of sentences can be used to express your thoughts. Make sure you use the correct punctuation at the end of your sentences so you don't confuse your reader.

Paragraphs

A **paragraph** is one or more sentences that tell about the same thing. All of the sentences go together to tell about one main idea.

Many paragraphs have a topic sentence, supporting sentences, and a closing sentence. A **topic sentence** tells the main idea. Often, the topic sentence is the first sentence in the paragraph. **Supporting sentences** tell more about the idea in the topic sentence. A closing sentence can be a summary, or it can provide a closing thought. With each new idea, a writer should begin a new paragraph. The first line of each paragraph is indented. This tells the reader where paragraphs begin and end.

Take a Look

Read this paragraph. The topic sentence is underlined. Notice how all of the sentences tell more about what makes Mona a good writer.

<u>Mona is a very good writer.</u> She uses a graphic organizer to plan her writing. Then she uses it to write a draft. After thinking about the draft for a day or two, Mona revises and edits it. Mona puts a lot of work into her writing.

Staying on Topic

All of the sentences in a paragraph should be about the same idea. If you include a sentence that doesn't belong in the paragraph, readers might get confused.

Take a Look

This paragraph doesn't stay on topic. The sentence that doesn't belong is crossed out. Read the paragraph with the sentence, then read it without.

Autumn is a beautiful time of year. ~~Spring is my favorite season.~~ On the first day of autumn, day is the same length as night. Later, leaves fall to the ground, and animals prepare for winter.

Try It!

Which sentence in this paragraph doesn't belong?

The first day of summer is June 20 or 21. It has more hours of daylight than any other day of the year. My birthday is in June. There are about 15 1/2 hours of daylight on the first day of summer.

Writing Paragraphs

You can write different kinds of paragraphs depending on your reason for writing. You might want to tell a story, describe something, explain something, or persuade someone.

Narrative

A **narrative** paragraph tells a story. The story can be real or make-believe. The purpose of a narrative paragraph is to entertain the reader.

Take a Look

Andrew wrote this narrative paragraph to put on the writer's bulletin board in his classroom.

Topic ▶ **Sentence**	I thought today was going to be the worst day of my life. I woke
Tell More ▶ **About Topic Sentence**	up late and couldn't find my shoes. When I went to eat breakfast, there was no milk. I had to put water on my cereal. Then I couldn't find my backpack, so I missed the
Closing ▶ **Sentence**	bus. Luckily, I had on my flying cape, and I made it to school before the bell rang. It turned out to be a pretty good day after all.

Descriptive

A **descriptive** paragraph describes something in a way that forms a picture in the reader's mind. Using words that tell how something looks, smells, feels, sounds, or tastes helps create the picture.

Take a Look

Here is Ethan's description of his dog.

> Oliver is a great friend to me. He's a white, tan, and black beagle. He likes to sleep under my bed. Every morning Oliver wakes me up by flapping his ears and jingling the tags on his collar. He also licks my face with his rough, wet tongue. Oliver's bad breath wakes me up in a hurry! Thanks to Oliver I'm never lonely at night or late for school in the morning.

◄ Topic Sentence

◄ Details: How Oliver Looks, Sounds, Feels, Smells

◄ Closing Sentence

Try It!

Think of your trip to school this morning. What did you see, smell, hear, feel, or taste along the way?

Expository

The purpose of an **expository** paragraph is to give information. It explains something that is real, not make-believe. Give examples or specific facts to make your ideas clear to your reader.

Take a Look

Read this paragraph that Gina wrote. Notice how she gives examples to support her topic sentence.

Topic Sentence ▶
Examples ▶
Closing Sentence ▶

Many different birds come to eat at our backyard birdfeeders. Yesterday I saw a cardinal, a blue jay, some sparrows, and a cowbird at our feeders. When the weather gets colder, even more kinds of birds will come.

Now read this paragraph that Shandra wrote about sharks. In this paragraph, she gives facts about sharks that tell more about her topic sentence.

Topic Sentence ▶
Facts ▶
Closing Sentence ▶

Sharks are very fast. Most of them swim 20 to 30 miles per hour. The mako shark can swim as fast as 60 miles per hour. Even the slowest shark can swim faster than a person can.

Persuasive

A **persuasive** paragraph gives the writer's view on a topic and reasons or examples to support it. The writer's purpose is to persuade the reader to agree with him or her.

Take a Look

Hanan wrote a persuasive paragraph for the school newspaper. She started with a question to interest her readers. Then, she answered the question in the rest of the paragraph.

> Why should we stop using foam food trays in the cafeteria? Every day about 400 kids eat a cafeteria lunch at our school. That means every day 400 foam trays are thrown away. They will be taken to a landfill. Foam trays never break down, so they will keep taking up more and more space. Trays that can be recycled or that will break down would be better choices.

◀ Question

◀ Support

◀ Closing Sentence

Reading Your Writing

Paragraphs can tell a story, describe, explain, or persuade. Use the kind of paragraph that fits your purpose for writing.

Graphic Organizers

A graphic organizer can be a useful tool for writers. You can use it during prewriting to gather your ideas and put them in order. There are many kinds of graphic organizers. Choose one that works with the type of writing you are doing, or create one of your own.

Story Map

This one is useful when you plan to write a story.

Title: The Bake Sale

Characters: Ben, Lucy, Ben's Mom, Ben's dog

Setting: The kitchen at Ben's house

Plot (What Happened)

Beginning (Problem): Ben and Lucy are supposed to bring three dozen cookies for a bake sale at their school.

Middle (Events):
1. Ben's mom helps him and Lucy bake the cookies.
2. Ben and Lucy let the cookies cool before icing them.
3. Ben and Lucy come back and see that Ben's dog has eaten all of the cookies.

Ending (How the problem was solved):
Ben and Lucy use their allowance money to buy cookies for the school bake sale.

Top-to-Bottom

This graphic organizer is useful when you are writing a description. It is called a **top-to-bottom** organizer.

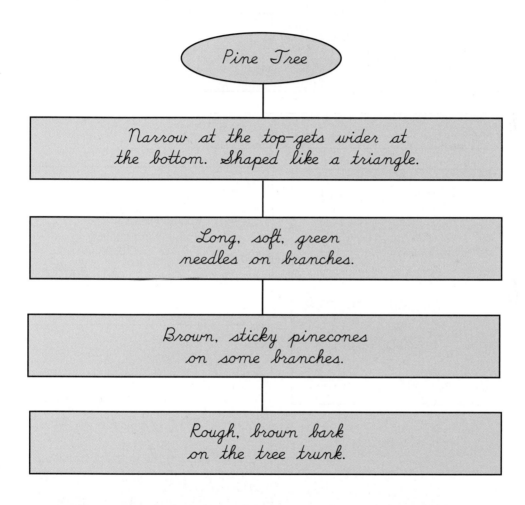

Try It!
Find an object in the classroom that you could describe from top-to-bottom. What would you put in the graphic organizer?

Writing a News Story

This graphic organizer is useful when you are writing a news story.

Headline
New Lights for Safe Nights

Byline   Tyra Jones

Who: City Council
What: New street lights
When: Next month
Where: Centerville
Why: Safer streets

Lead
City Council agrees to pay for new street lights.

Body
Lights will be put up on streets in Centerville starting next month. Project will take about 6 months to complete.

Ending
New lights make streets look nice, people feel safe.

Venn Diagram

This graphic organizer is useful when you are comparing and contrasting two things. It is called a **Venn diagram.**

Soccer   *Baseball*

Different

Ball is kicked

Only goalie can touch ball with hands

Playing time is divided into halves

Alike

Sport

Played by teams

Different

Ball is hit with bat

Any player can throw ball with hands

Playing time divided into innings

Reading Your Writing
Graphic organizers help you make a plan for your writing. Taking the time to collect and organize your ideas will make what you write easier to read.

Fun Fact

The Venn diagram was named after John Venn, a mathematician from England.

Writer's Craft

People read what you write. You want them to enjoy your letters, stories, and poems. You want them to learn from your reports and descriptions. You can help them. Here are some ways to make your writing better.

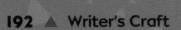

Purpose and Audience

You can call your cousin on the phone. You can talk to a friend at school. You can write a letter to your grandmother. These are all ways to communicate with another person.

Writing is a special way to communicate because the people you write can save what you write and read it again. You can also plan what you want to say and change it before you send your letter.

The three most important things to think about when you write are **what, why,** and **who.**

1. *What* is the topic you want to write about.
2. *Why* is your **purpose** for writing. You can *entertain, inform, explain,* and *persuade* with writing.
3. *Who* is the **audience** that will read your writing. You can change what you write about and the words you use to fit your audience.

Good writers communicate their thoughts well. They do this by keeping their audience and purpose in mind while they are planning, writing, and changing their writing.

Danielle likes to make up stories to entertain her four-year-old brother, Marty. She thought of one while he was sleeping. Danielle started to write her story down so she wouldn't forget it.

Once upon a time, there was a boy named Marty who had a giant bird for a friend. The bird's name was Swifty. He was just the right size to take Marty for rides.

When everyone else was asleep, Swifty would come and take Marty for a ride. Every night they would fly to a different place!

Last night, Swifty and Marty flew to Alaska. They saw whales and polar bears. Then they saw a pirate ship. Marty warned the people in the town. He saved them from the pirates.

The purpose of Danielle's story is to entertain. She likes to tell Marty stories to make him smile.

Danielle knows her audience very well, so she picked a subject that he likes. She knows that Marty likes birds and loves to hear stories about himself. Because Marty is just four years old, Danielle doesn't use big words or long sentences.

Ryan wanted to tell his grandmother about his winning goal in the soccer game. He decided to write her a letter.

> 1735 Juniper Way
> Boaz, Alabama 35957
> September 8, 2003
>
> Dear Grandma,
>   We played our first soccer game on Saturday, and guess what? I got the only goal in the whole game!
>   It was almost the end of the game when I finally got the ball. I ran all the way up the field and past all the other players! I made a fake move to the right. When the goalie moved to follow my fake, I kicked and scored!
>   You should've been there, Grandma. Everyone was jumping up and down and cheering. I hope you can come see one of my games. If you do, be sure to wear your jumping shoes!
>   Love,
>   Ryan

Ryan's purpose was to inform his grandmother about his winning goal in the soccer game. Ryan's audience was his grandmother. He knew she would like to know about his goal.

Try It!

Match each writing purpose and topic with an audience.

Entertain with fishing stories and jokes	Students, Teachers
Persuade to serve pizza once a week	3rd Grade Class
Inform about new books in library	Friend
Explain how to fly a kite	School Officials

Here are three ways thinking about your audience and purpose will help you stay in touch with your readers.

1. **Ideas:** Different ideas and topics will be interesting to different audiences. Be sure to pick a topic that will interest your readers.

2. **Word Choice:** Different words are used when writing for different age groups. Check to make sure your readers are able to understand what you write.

3. **Voice:** Different voices are used for different purposes. Use a friendly voice to entertain and a polite voice to explain.

Reading Your Writing

Take time to decide on your audience and purpose before you begin writing. You will be more successful in communicating with your reader.

Time and Order Words

Time words tell when things happen. *Last night, this morning, yesterday, tomorrow, next Saturday,* and *today* are time words.

Order words tell in what order things happen. *First, then, next, after, later,* and *finally* are order words.

Time and order words help you organize your writing and make your writing easier to follow and understand.

Take a Look

Amy wrote in her journal about her trip to her grandparents' farm. She used time words to help organize her story.

> Last month my family took a trip to my grandparents' farm. We left early in the morning so we could get there by dinnertime. Dad had to drive all day Friday. Then he slept all day Saturday! We had planned to stay until the next weekend, and we almost did.
>
> Mom's hay fever started right away, though. Then, my little brother broke his arm on Monday. Every morning at 5:00 a.m., the roosters woke us up. Dad said we had to go home before anything else happened!

Jeremy wrote about a science project in his class. Here is part of his report. He used order words to help organize his explanation.

> First we got a tall jar and made a papier-mâché mountain around it. After the mountain was dry, we painted it. Then we glued twigs on it to look like trees. Finally, we were ready to explode the volcano.

Try It!

There are time and order words in the sentences below. See if you can find them all.

Last year I was in the second grade, and I was the shortest kid in my class. This week, we finally got a new kid who is shorter than I am!

Reading Your Writing

Knowing words that show time and order will help you keep track of the order of events as you write. Using these signal words will also help make your writing easier to follow and understand.

Place and Location Words

Place and **location** words show where people or things are. These words can also show where the action is happening. *Above, across, at, behind, below, beside, between, by, down, in, next to, on, over, through, up*, and *under* are place and location words.

We took the long way home today.
We took the long way, down the road beside the river and through the woods, to get home today.

The first sentence tells just a fact. The second sentence uses place and location words to give a clear picture of *the long way home.*

Take a Look

Tara wrote a newspaper article about helping pack the car for a family camping trip. She used place and location words to tell where everything was.

Pack It Up!

Here's how to pack a car for a camping trip. First we pack the backpacks in the back. Sleeping bags go on top of the backpacks. We put the tent over the sleeping bags. Games and books are packed under the seats.

Try It!

What place and location words can you add to the two sentences below to make them clearer?

under the table   *across the street*
behind the sofa   *up in the tree*
on the shelf   *in a box*

I looked for my kitten.

I finally found her.

Using place and location words helps you communicate with your readers in two ways.

Ideas: Place and location words help give readers a clear picture of where people, things, and actions are.

Word Choice: Choosing the right place and location words helps readers understand your writing.

Reading Your Writing

You can use words that show place and location as you write to show where people or things are or where something is happening. This will help your readers understand your writing.

Effective Beginnings and Endings

An **effective beginning** in writing is one that grabs your readers' attention and makes them want to read more. Think about the beginnings of your favorite books and stories. What about them grabbed your attention?

Take a Look

Here are four ways to write effective beginnings for stories and plays.

▶ Ask a question.

> *If you could go anywhere, where would you go? Most kids might pick a theme park. Howard wants to go to the moon!*

▶ Use details that describe sight, sound, taste, smell, or touch. Put the reader into the scene.

> *Tony whistled as he rode his bike down Third Avenue. It was a cool October morning. He could smell smoke from a wood-burning stove. As he came to the last house on his route, he saw a strange glow in one of the windows.*

▶ Use dialogue (speaker's word in quotation marks).

> *"Watch out!" someone shouted. I turned around. "Oh, no!" I said. "Here comes trouble!"*

▶ Tell about a problem.

> *My ruler, an eraser, and now one glove were missing from my backpack. Every day something new was gone.*

More Effective Beginnings

Here are four ways to write effective beginnings for book reviews, news stories, and informational reports.

▶ Ask a question.

Who planted all of those flowers? Ms. Cameron's third grade class did! They planted them at recess on Thursday.

▶ Tell something that happened to a person.

My older sister Karen works for an animal doctor. People are always giving her kittens. Now we have 12 cats at home!

▶ Use an interesting or surprising fact.

Smiling is easier than frowning. Only about 17 muscles are used to smile. It takes about 43 muscles to frown.

▶ Tell about a problem.

We get only 20 minutes to eat lunch. By the time we get our food and sit down, it's almost time to go.

Writing effective beginnings is one of the best ways to get and hold readers' attention. Try one of these ideas the next time you start writing.

Effective Endings

An **effective ending** brings your writing to a close and keeps the reader thinking about it.

Here are three ways to end reports and articles.

▶ Sum up the subject.

Kids should be astronauts. They are small and use less food, water, and air. It's time they had a chance to travel in space.

▶ Use a quote as Judith E. Rinard did in her article "Kids Did It! in Business."

Abbey and her dad designed and perfected "Makin' Bacon." "I'm proud I thought of it," says Abbey.

▶ Request action.

When you see litter on the ground, please pick it up! You may save an animal's life.

Here are two ways to end stories.
▶ Use an interesting idea.

Food that the kids didn't eat could be used for compost.

▶ Use surprise or humor.

Beth carefully lifted the lid and looked inside the box. She saw the cutest little puppy she'd ever seen.

▶ Using Dialogue

Dialogue is two or more people talking to each other in a story. Characters seem real when their own words show how they think and feel. Dialogue can also help the action of the story move along quickly.

Writers use quotation marks to show the words that the characters speak. When you use quotation marks, readers will know someone is speaking.

Take a Look

In *Angel Child, Dragon Child*, Michele Maria Surat uses dialogue to move her story along and show the characters' thoughts and feelings. The school principal has just stopped a fight between two students.

> *"We can't have this fighting. You two have to help each other," ordered the principal. He pointed at me. "Hoa, you need to speak to Raymond. Use our words. Tell him about Vietnam." Raymond glared. "And you, Raymond, you must learn to listen. You will write Hoa's story."*

Look at the example of dialogue you just read. Notice the paragraph indent. This was a signal that the principal began to speak. That makes it easier for the reader to tell who is talking. Speaker tags, a group of words beginning with a person's name and a word like *said*, *asked*, or *answered*, help too.

Try It!

Match the dialogue quote with the speaker tag.

▶ *"You can play basketball in a wheelchair?"*

▶ *"Just watch me!"*

● *Jason answered as he stole the ball and sped off.*

● *Nancy asked as she caught the ball.*

Reading Your Writing

Dialogue can add interest to your story and help make your characters seem real. You can also tell part of the story through dialogue.

Making Comparisons

Writers sometimes **compare** very different things to make colorful pictures in readers' minds. **Similes, metaphors,** and **personification** are three ways writers make comparisons with things that are not alike.

▶ **Similes** use the words *like* or *as* to compare things.

▶ **Metaphors** compare things without stating that's what they're doing.

▶ **Personification** describes animals or things as if they were people.

Similes use *like* or *as*.

> *She was as light as a feather.*
>
> *They fought like cats and dogs.*

Metaphors don't use *like* or *as*.

> *My feet were blocks of ice.*
>
> *When she walked on stage, her legs turned to rubber.*

Personification talks about animals or things as if they were people.

> *The curtains of the old house kept their secrets well.*
>
> *The wind whispered to the trees.*

Try It!

Identify whether the following sentences use similes, metaphors, or personification.

William is a history book; he knows everything about the Second World War.

Margaret sings like a bird.

Reading Your Writing

Look for similes, metaphors, and personification in the poems and stories you read. Then try writing some of your own. By adding similes, metaphors, and personification to your writing, you will make your writing more interesting and fun to read.

Many famous children's books have been written about animals that act like people. The animals even know how to spell in *Charlotte's Web.* The story by E. B. White is the best-selling paperback book for kids.

Using the Sounds of Words

Writers often use words for **sounds** as well as for meaning. Carefully choosing words that sound good together helps make your writing richer and more descriptive.

Take a Look

Here are four ways writers of stories and poems use the sounds of words in their writing.

▶ **End Rhyme:** Poets often use rhyming words at the ends of their lines of poetry.

> *Houses are faces*
> *(haven't you **found?**)*
> *with their hats in the air,*
> *and their necks in the **ground**.*
> —from "Houses" by Aileen Fisher

▶ **Onomatopoeia:** This is using a word that spells the sound something makes.

> *The bee **buzzed** around the flower.*

▶ **Alliteration:** This is using several words with the same beginning consonant sound.

> *The **cat crept carefully** across the **carpet.***

▶ **Repetition of Words:** Writers repeat words when they want to make a strong statement.

> ***Long, long*** *ago, before airplanes and rockets, my great-grandmother dreamed of going to the moon.*

Try It!

What do each of the following sentences use: onomatopoeia, alliteration, or repetition of words?

> *Danny didn't demand dessert after dinner.*

> *Zing, bang, crackle, pop! The Fourth of July was going off everywhere!*

> *I've thought about you many, many times since I saw you last.*

Reading Your Writing

Using words for their sounds as well as their meanings can make your stories and poems more vivid and descriptive. Look for examples of end rhyme, alliteration, onomatopoeia, and repetition of words in the poems and stories you read. Then try using them in your own writing.

Many actors and announcers use tongue twisters to practice speaking clearly. See if you can say each of these fast three times:
Greek grapes
Pug puppy
Toy boat

Sentence Combining

   If your writing has short, choppy sentences, it will sound smoother if you make sentences different lengths. You can do this by **combining** some of the sentences.

   The conjunctions *and*, *but*, and *or* can be used to combine different types of sentences.

▶ *And* is used to combine sentences with similar ideas.

▶ *But* is used to combine sentences with opposite or contrasting ideas.

▶ *Or* is used to combine sentences that give choices.

Take a Look

   Use *and* for sentences with similar ideas.

> *I called Mary on the phone. We talked about books.*
>
> **Better:** *I called Mary on the phone, **and** we talked about books.*

   Use *but* for sentences with opposite ideas.

> *The dog seemed friendly. It might bite someone.*
>
> **Better:** *The dog seemed friendly, **but** it might bite someone.*

   Use *or* for sentences that give choices.

> *Do you want to play? Do you have to go home now?*
>
> **Better:** *Do you want to play, **or** do you have to go home now?*

Try It!

Combine each pair of sentences with *and*, *but*, or *or*. Don't forget the comma.

> I like these three movies. I don't have time to watch them all.

> My family went to the beach. We swam all afternoon.

> I could buy pizza now. I could save my dollar.

Reading Your Writing

Try combining some of your short, choppy sentences. Think about how the sentences are related. That will help you know which conjunction to use. Don't forget to put a comma before the conjunction. Your writing will be smoother and easier to understand.

Ways to Develop Expository Writing

Expository writing explains or gives information about a topic. Expository writing can be a report about sharks, an article for the school newspaper about recycling, or directions for getting from one place to another.

There are different ways to develop expository writing. You start with the main idea. Then you choose what kinds of details you are going to use to support it. You might use examples, reasons or causes, or facts.

Using Examples

Giving examples is good when ideas are hard to understand. Good examples will help your readers understand the ideas.

Take a Look

Read the paragraph below. The main idea is in the first sentence. The other two sentences give examples to support the main idea.

Some of the largest animals in the world live in Africa. The African elephant can be 12 feet high and weigh up to 8,000 pounds. Giraffes can be 20 feet tall.

Pictures as Examples

Another way to give examples is to add photographs or drawings. For example, a map would be a good way to give someone directions for getting from one place to another.

Try It!

Match each main idea with the examples that would help explain or tell about it.

Main Ideas

There is a pet that is right for every person.

Rainy Saturdays can be lots of fun.

Examples

Have a paper airplane flying contest in the hall.

Dogs are good pets if you like to walk.

Have an indoor picnic.

If you're busy, a goldfish is a good pet.

Reading Your Writing

Using examples in your expository writing helps explain your ideas. You can use words and pictures to do this. When you use examples, your ideas will be clearer to your readers.

Using Reasons or Causes

Writers use **reasons** and **causes** to explain more about the main idea. Reasons and causes tell why things happen, why people feel as they do, or why things are the way they are.

Take a Look

Gina wrote about her favorite season—fall. She used reasons to explain why fall is the best season of all. Gina wrote an effective ending by putting her best reason last.

> Fall, the Best of All!
>
> By Gina Leonardo
>
> Fall is the very best time of year. Fall is not too hot, like summer, and not too cold, like winter. It is just the right temperature. Fall is the prettiest season because the leaves change color. It is so much fun to jump into piles of leaves. Best of all, my birthday is right in the middle of fall!

Try It!

Match each main idea with a reason or cause.

Main Ideas

Schools should serve an afternoon snack.

Students should help make classroom rules.

Reasons or Causes

Students would obey rules they helped make.

Students could do better work in the afternoon.

Reasons and causes can help you organize your writing. First, write your main idea. Next, make a list of the reasons or causes you want to use. Put them in order of their importance to you. Save your best one for last. Then, use your list to develop your main idea.

Reading Your Writing

Reasons and causes are a way to give more information about a main idea. They answer the "why" questions about a main idea.

Using Facts

Many writers use **facts** when writing reports and articles. Facts are details that are known to be true. Using facts gives your readers more information and helps them believe what you are telling them.

Read the paragraph below. Look for important facts.

The stars and the stripes on the United States flag both mean something. There are fifty white stars on a blue background. They stand for the fifty states. The thirteen red and white stripes stand for the original thirteen colonies.

In this paragraph, the writer states that both the stars and the stripes on the United States flag mean something. That is the main idea. Then, the writer gives important facts that tell what the stars and stripes mean. These facts help readers understand and believe the main idea.

Try It!

Which of the facts listed below would help readers understand and believe the main idea?

Whales come in different sizes.

Facts
▶ Beluga whales grow to about 14 feet long.
▶ Killer whales can often be seen at sea animal parks.
▶ Killer whales can be about 30 feet long.
▶ The blue whale is the largest mammal in the world.
▶ Whales can communicate with each other.

Reading Your Writing

Use facts to make your writing more believable. Facts also make it easier for your readers to understand. As you read, watch for examples of how writers use facts to support their ideas. When you write, use facts to tell readers more about your ideas.

Ingredients for Writing a Story

The ingredients, or parts, of a story are **characters, plot, setting,** and **point of view.** These four pages will tell you how to use them to write a story.

Characters

Characters are people in the story. Writers make their characters seem like real people by describing to the reader what the characters do, say, think, and feel.

▶ **Just Telling the Facts:** *Stephanie sat on the bench.*

▶ **Making a Character Seem Real:** *Stephanie sat on the bench, ready to join the game at any moment.*

Setting

Setting is the time and place in which the story happens. The author can help the reader understand the setting by describing what the characters see, feel, hear, and smell.

If a story has different settings, writers must let readers know when they change the time or place.

▶ **Character Helps Tell About the Setting:** *"Look at that sunset!" she said, looking out over the ocean.*

▶ **Setting Changes:** *By the end of summer, Greg's family had moved from New York City to Wyoming.*

Plot

Plot is what happens in a story. The plot tells about a problem and how the characters solve it.

The plot has three parts: a **beginning, middle,** and **end.**

▶ The beginning tells about a problem the characters have.

▶ The middle tells how the characters struggle with the problem. The story builds to a "high point" just before the problem is solved.

▶ The end tells how the problem is solved.

Point of View

The **point of view** is who is telling the story. In the **first-person** point of view, a character in the story tells the story. The first-person storyteller uses the words *I, me, we,* and *us*.

In the **third-person** point of view, the storyteller describes things that happen to other people. The third-person storyteller uses the words *he, she, him, her, they,* and *them*.

Reuben Pearce thought it would be fun to write *Little Red Riding Hood* from the wolf's **point of view.**

My Side of the Story

One afternoon in the woods, I saw a girl wearing a red cloak, and I stopped to talk to her. She was going to her grandma's house for pizza. I love pizza. I was hoping she would invite me over. She didn't.

I ran ahead to Grandma's. A note on the door said that Grandma was walking her dog.

I was in the kitchen when I heard the girl with the red cloak call out, "Grandma!" I put an apron around my tummy and a dish towel on my head.

"The pizza's not ready," I said in a high, creaky voice. "Come back later, dear."

"You don't sound anything like Grandma," the girl said, walking into the kitchen.

The last thing I remember was her hand coming toward my nose.

I woke up in this cage—not a fun place for a wolf. Here's my advice to all you wolves out there: "Stay far, far away from girls in red cloaks!"

Try It!
What is the point of view in Reuben's story? How do you know?

Looking for Setting, Characters, and Plot

Look at Reuben's story again. He tells the setting in the first sentence. The time is afternoon and the place is the woods. The setting changes later in the story.

Both characters are introduced in the first paragraph. Reuben lets you know what the wolf says, does, and thinks and what the little girl says and does.

The plot of the story begins with the problem. The wolf wants some pizza. The events in the story show how the wolf tried to get some pizza. The story ends when the wolf doesn't get any pizza. He ends up in a cage instead.

Reading Your Writing
A good story has characters that seem real. It has a plot with a beginning, middle, and end. The plot has a problem and a solution. The story has a setting and a point of view. Use these ingredients when you write to make your stories interesting for your readers.

Vocabulary

Each word has its own meaning. Writers carefully choose the words they use. They want words to communicate exactly what they want to say. When that happens, their writing comes alive for readers. You can make the same choices when you write. Learning about different kinds of words will help.

Compound Words

A **compound word** is made by putting two words together to form one word. Sometimes you can figure out the meaning of a compound word by looking at the two words that form it.

every + one = everyone

A compound word doesn't always take its meaning from the words that form it.

under + stand = understand

high + way = highway

Try It!

Name a compound word that could replace each of the phrases below.

▶ house for a dog
▶ coat you wear in the rain
▶ knob on a door
▶ corn made for popping

Writing Connection

A compound word is made by joining two smaller words. Look in a dictionary to make sure the compound word you are using is spelled correctly.

Antonyms

An **antonym** is a word that means the opposite or nearly the opposite of another word. Words such as *hot* and *cold* are antonyms.

You can use antonyms in your writing to show a difference between two things.

Here are some antonyms you might use in your writing.

right—left	*early—late*	*before—after*
wild—tame	*close—open*	*wet—dry*
lost—found	*rough—smooth*	*short—long*

Try It!
Think of an antonym for each word below.

full   day   push

Writing Connection
Antonyms are words with opposite meanings. Use antonyms to point out differences.

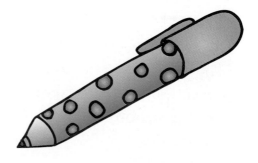

Synonyms

A **synonym** is a word that has the same or almost the same meaning as another word. The words *sad, unhappy,* and *gloomy* are synonyms.

When you use the same words again and again, your readers can become bored. Using different words to say the same thing or to make your message clearer helps keep your reader interested. Here is an example:

Instead of saying: *Jasmine saw a big spider.*
You might say: *Jasmine saw an enormous spider.*

Here are some other synonyms you could use in your writing.

hard—difficult	*task—chore*	*yell—shout*
seem—appear	*story—tale*	*right—correct*
sick—ill	*mistake—error*	*cry—weep*

Try It!
Think of a synonym for each of these words.
happy   angry   tired

Writing Connection
Synonyms are words with similar meanings. Using synonyms helps make your writing more interesting.

Adjectives

An **adjective** is a word that adds information to a noun or a pronoun. Adjectives tell how something looks, feels, smells, sounds, or tastes. They also tell how many or how much. Using adjectives helps your reader imagine what you are describing.

Good: *I have a pencil.*

Better: *I have a **shiny blue** pencil with a **sharp** point.*

Here are some other adjectives you might use in your writing.

Looks	Smells	Tastes	Sounds	Feels
small	sweet	sour	squeaky	wet
green	stinky	spicy	quiet	slimy
round	clean	bitter	clanging	smooth
bright	musty	sweet	noisy	fuzzy

Try It!
Think of adjectives to describe a pizza.

Writing Connection
An adjective adds information to a noun or pronoun. Adjectives can help your reader picture or sense the things you describe.

Homophones

Homophones are words that sound the same but have different spellings and meanings. Words such as *ate* and *eight* are homophones. *Ate* is the past tense of *eat*. *Eight* is a number that is one more than seven.

Knowing the meanings of homophones will help you choose the correct words when you are writing.

If you are not sure which spelling is the right one, look up the words in a dictionary and read their meanings.

Here is a list of homophones and their meanings. Notice how each one is used in a sentence.

by—near *buy*—to pay for something	*The room is* by *the library.* *I will* buy *my lunch today.*
hear—to listen *here*—at or in this place	*I* hear *someone singing.* *Will you be* here *tomorrow?*
hole—an opening *whole*—entire	*I have a* hole *in my shoe.* *I ate the* whole *sandwich.*
right—correct; right direction *write*—make marks on paper	*The car turned* right. *I will* write *a story.*
their—possessive pronoun *there*—at another place *they're*—they are	*What is* their *last name?* *Put the box over* there. They're *leaving now.*
to—in the direction of *too*—also; very *two*—number	*Throw* to *first base.* *I want to go* too. *I am* too *hot.* *I have* two *books.*
your—possessive pronoun *you're*—you are	*Are these* your *pencils?* You're *my best friend.*
its—possessive pronoun *it's*—it is	*The bird is in* its *cage.* It's *singing sweetly.*

Try It!

Think of sentences using the homophones *pear* and *pair*.

Writing Connection

Homophones sound the same but have different meanings and spellings. Look up a homophone in the dictionary to make sure you use the correct word. Choosing the wrong homophone could confuse your readers.

Words with More Than One Meaning

Many words are spelled the same but have more than one meaning. For example, a *bat* can be a flying animal or it may be a stick used to hit a baseball. Here are some more words that are spelled and sound the same but have different meanings.

batter—one who hits a ball	*batter*—liquid cake mixture
fly—an insect	*fly*—go through the air
bill—money owed	*bill*—bird's beak
gum—sticky stuff from trees	*gum*—body tissue around teeth
ear—body part used for hearing	*ear*—part of a corn plant
story—something you read or tell	*story*—a level of a building
fan—machine for moving air	*fan*—a supporter of a sports team

When you are writing, be sure to give your readers enough information to know which word you are using. For example, if you write *I saw a fan,* it is not clear which fan you mean. If you give your reader more information by writing *I saw a fan yelling during the game,* then your reader knows you mean someone who supports a team.

More Words with More Than One Meaning

Some words that are spelled the same are both pronounced differently and mean different things. For example, *bow* can be pronounced with a long *o* sound and mean "a ribbon on a package." It can rhyme with *cow* and mean "to bend from the waist."

Here are some words you might use in your writing.

live (long *i*)—having life *live* (short *i*)—to exist	That is a *live* frog. Do you *live* here?
wind (long *i*)—to turn *wind* (short *i*)—moving air	*Wind* the clock. The *wind* blew.

Try It!
Make up sentences using some of the words above to show their meaning.

Writing Connection
Be aware of words that are spelled the same but have different meanings. They may be pronounced the same way or differently. When you use them in your writing, it is important to give your reader enough information to know which word you are using.

▶ Prefixes

A **prefix** is a word part added to the beginning of a word, changing the meaning. The prefix *re-* means "again." Adding *re-* to the base word *write* makes the word *rewrite*, which means "to write again."

Some prefixes have more than one meaning. Here are some common prefixes and their meanings.

Prefix	Meaning	Example
re-	again	repaint
un-	not, opposite, reverse action	unhappy, unable, unlock
dis-	not, opposite	disagree
mis-	bad or wrong	misspell
over-	too much	overcooked
bi-	two	bicycle
tri-	three	triangle
pre-	before	preschool

Try It!

What prefix would you add to *appear* to make a word that means "to appear again"?

Writing Connection

A prefix is added to the beginning of a word and changes its meaning. Learning and using prefixes will help you add to your vocabulary.

Suffixes

A **suffix** is a word part that is added to the end of a word and changes its meaning. For example, the suffix -ful means "full of." Adding -ful to the base word fear makes the word fearful, which means "full of fear."

Use suffixes to make words that tell the reader exactly what you want to say. Here are some suffixes and their meanings.

Suffix	Meaning	Example
-ful	full of	joyful
-less	without	careless
-er, -or	one who does	teacher, actor
-ness	state or quality of	darkness
-y	being or having	dirty
-ly	like	fatherly

Try It!

Combine each base word and suffix. What is the meaning of the new word?

hope + ful   honest + ly   work + er

Writing Connection

A suffix is added to the end of a word and changes its meaning. If you aren't sure what a suffix means, look it up in the dictionary.

Context Clues

How do you figure out the meaning of a new word that you find when you are reading? One way is to use **context clues.** Context clues are found in the words and sentences near the unfamiliar word. Pictures can also give context clues that help you figure out a word's meaning.

Look at this example from the story *Sarah, Plain and Tall* by Patricia MacLachlan.

"Cold in town," said Papa. "And Jack was feisty." Jack was Papa's horse that he'd raised from a colt. "Rascal," murmured Papa, smiling, because no matter what Jack did Papa loved him.

You may not know what the word *feisty* means, but there are clues in the sentences that follow it if you don't. Papa calls him a rascal, so we know that his behavior isn't always good. We also find out that Papa will love Jack no matter what he does. That makes us think Jack did something that might make someone mad.

Sometimes context clues come right after the word. Here is an example about rats from *The City Kid's Field Guide* by Ethan Herberman called "City Superheroes." The words that follow *nocturnal* tell what it means.

"Does it help to be 'nocturnal'—to be active at night?"

Here's another example from *Sarah, Plain and Tall* by Patricia MacLachlan. Use context clues to figure out what Seal might be. Tell what clues you used.

". . . She turned and lifted a black case from the wagon. 'And Seal, too.'

Carefully she opened the case, and Seal, gray with white feet, stepped out. Lottie lay down, her head on her paws, staring. Nick leaned down to sniff. Then he lay down, too."

Tips for Understanding New Words

▶ Keep reading. Look for clues in the words and sentences near the new word.

▶ Look for context clues in pictures.

Writing Connection

Context clues help a reader figure out the meaning of a new word. Include context clues in your writing if you use words that readers might not know.

Across-the-Curriculum Words

You will probably read many new words in books about math, science, social studies, and health. Learning these words will help you understand what you read. You can also use them in your writing.

Here is a list of words you might find in these subjects. A definition is given for each word.

Math

addition—combining numbers into one sum
decimal—relating to or based on the number *ten*
difference—the number that is left after subtracting one quantity from another
divide—to separate or arrange into groups
estimate—to make a rough judgment or calculation of
fraction—one or more of the equal parts of a whole
graph—a diagram showing the changes of and relationship between two or more elements
order—to arrange by size or amount
place value—the value given to a digit, based on the position it has in a number
sum—the answer obtained from adding numbers

Science

amphibian—cold-blooded vertebrates (including frogs, toads, and salamanders) usually living in or near water

cell—the basic unit of all living things

dissolve—to cause to pass into solution with a liquid

energy—the ability to do work

erosion—the gradual wearing or washing away of the soil and rock of the earth's surface by glaciers, waves, running water, or wind

friction—the force that resists motion between two surfaces that are touching

gravity—the force that the earth exerts on bodies at or near its surface

hypothesis—an unproved explanation based on known facts

recycle—to use again

Social Studies

artifact—something made and left behind by people who lived long ago

barter—to trade (goods or services) without using money

Capitol—the building in Washington, D.C., where the U.S. Congress meets

consumer—a person who buys goods and services

country—a nation or independent state

culture—the way of life of a group of people, including their common language, social institutions, customs, beliefs, and art

equator—an imaginary line around the center of the earth halfway between the North and South Poles

explorer—a person who travels to collect information about geography or science

producer—a person or group that makes goods or provides services

rural—relating to the country or country life

urban—relating to a city or city life

Health

bacteria—a one-celled organism that may help or hurt
its host

digestion—the process by which food is broken down
and used by the body

disease—illness

infection—an attack on part of the body by bacteria,
viruses, or fungi whose growth causes
disease

medicine—a drug or other substance used to treat
disease or relieve pain

stress—mental or physical tension or pressure

Try It!

Use one word from each subject area in a sentence.

Writing Connection

Learning words that are used in different subjects
can help you better understand what you read. You
might also use these words when you write your
own stories and reports.

Rules of Writing: Grammar, Usage, and Mechanics

You know about rules. When you know and follow the rules of a game, you're better at the game. It's the same with writing. Knowing the rules and following them will make you a better writer.

Grammar

Grammar is about how language is organized. Parts of speech, such as nouns and verbs, are grammar. The names for different parts of a sentence are grammar. Knowing about grammar helps you understand how to build sentences that make sense to your readers.

Nouns

Nouns name everything. For example, **nouns** are words that name people, places, things, and ideas.

boy   zoo   balloons   time

Common nouns name any person, place, thing, or idea. Common nouns start with a lowercase letter. **Proper nouns** name specific persons, places, things, or ideas. Proper nouns start with a capital letter.

Common nouns: girl, park, skyscraper, nationality

Proper nouns: Megan, Yellowstone Park, Sears Tower, Cuban

Singular and Plural Nouns

A **singular noun** names one. A **plural noun** names more than one.

▶ **Regular plural nouns** are formed by adding *-s*, *-es*, or *-ies* to singular nouns.

dog **dogs**   box **boxes**   baby **babies**

▶ **Irregular plural nouns** do not follow the rules for forming regular plural nouns. There are no rules for forming irregular plural nouns. Check the dictionary for the correct spelling of irregular plural nouns. Below are some examples.

child **children**   tooth **teeth**
man **men**   deer **deer**

Possessive Nouns

Possessive nouns show who has or owns something.

Grandpa's blue eyes   the **raccoon's** tail
a **firefighter's** hat   the **room's** doors

Singular possessive nouns are formed by adding an apostrophe (') plus *s* to singular nouns. **Plural possessive nouns** can be formed in two ways. When a plural noun ends with *s*, an apostrophe is added to form the possessive plural noun. When a plural noun does not end with *s*, an apostrophe plus *s* is added to form the possessive plural noun.

Singular Possessive Nouns

robin + 's = robin's   the **robin's** nest

Plural Possessive Nouns

players + ' = players'   the **players'** baseball gloves
women + 's = women's   the **women's** offices

Try It!

Which of the five possessive nouns in the sentence below are singular? Which are plural?

Tyler's dad brought the students' sweaters from the teacher's van to the third graders' bench at the Children's Kite-Flying Contest.

Pronouns

Pronouns are words that take the place of nouns. Personal pronouns refer to people or things.

Olivia loves to swim.	**She** loves to swim.
Yusef bought **the poster.**	Yusef bought **it.**
The Lions won the game.	**They** won the game.
Mustafa brought **Tracie and me** a pizza.	Mustafa brought **us** a pizza.

Pronouns can be singular or plural.

Singular	I, me, you, he, him, she, her, it
Plural	we, us, they, them, you

Tyler (singular noun) likes to ride *his bike* (singular noun).

He (singular pronoun) likes to ride *it* (singular pronoun).

My sisters (plural noun) like to play with *Sam* (singular noun).

They (plural pronoun) like to play with *him* (singular pronoun).

Try It!

Find the five personal pronouns in the sentences below.

I wanted to go to the movies, but they didn't. She thought you were with us.

Possessive Pronouns

A **possessive pronoun** shows who owns something. Possessive pronouns take the place of possessive nouns and can be singular or plural. Possessive pronouns do not have apostrophes. Some possessive pronouns are used before nouns. Others are used alone.

children's song	**Jane's** brother	**Min's** book
their song	**her** brother	**his** book
our cat	**my** bike	**their** car
the cat is **ours**	the bike is **mine**	the car is **theirs**

Here are all of the singular and plural possessive pronouns.

	Used Before Nouns	Used Alone
Singular	my your its her his	mine yours its hers his
Plural	our their your	ours theirs yours

Try It!

There are three possessive pronouns in the sentences below. Can you find them all?

My book is red, and her book is blue. Kevin thought the blue one was mine.

Verbs

There are different types of verbs. An **action verb** tells about an action of something or someone in a sentence. Actions can be seen or unseen.

Seen action: The dog **ran** all the way home.

Unseen action: Alex **forgot** his library book.

A **state-of-being verb** does not tell about an action. It tells about a condition or a state of being.

Our friends **were** here for a visit.

When a state-of-being verb connects the subject of a sentence with a word in the predicate, the verb is a **linking verb.**

I **am** a student.   My aunt **is** a teacher.

You **are** a good cook.   Josh **was** helpful with the baby.

A **verb phrase** is one or more **helping verbs** followed by the **main verb.** Helping verbs help the main verb express an action or state of being.

She **has won** the race. (helping verb+main verb)

She **could have won** the race. (two helping verbs+main verb)

Forms of *Be* and *Have*

The verb **be** does not show the action of someone or something in a sentence. It is a state-of-being verb. It tells what someone or something is or is like. There are different forms of the verb *be*.

am   are   is   was   were   being   been

Forms of *be* can be used as linking verbs.

The team **is** unbeaten.

The dog **was** lost.

The Carson twins **were** my friends.

Forms of *be* can also be used as helping verbs and as main verbs.

I **am** walking. (helping verb)

They **were** writing. (helping verb)

She has **been** here. (main verb)

The verb **have** can be used as a main verb or as a helping verb.

have   has   had

She **has** a kitten. (main verb)

The kittens **have become** playful. (helping verb)

My mother **has decided** to keep them. (helping verb)

Adjectives and Adverbs

Adjectives describe a noun or a pronoun. Adjectives tell what kind, how many, and which one.

What Kind	How Many	Which One
blue	three	this
long	many	that
furry	few	these
good	some	those

Proper adjectives are made from proper nouns. Like proper nouns, proper adjectives always start with a capital letter.

American flag   *Chinese* food   *Spanish* folksongs

Articles

Articles are a special group of adjectives. *A* and *an* are **indefinite articles.** They refer to a general group of people, places, things, or ideas.

A is used before words that begin with a consonant sound.   *a* dog   *a* house   *a* card

An is used before words that begin with a vowel sound.

an egg   *an* hour   *an* apple

The is a **definite article.** It identifies specific people, places, things, or ideas.

the book   *the* door   *the* cat

Adverbs

An **adverb** is a word that describes a verb, an adjective, or another adverb. An adverb tells how, when, where, or how much something happens.

How	When	Where	How Much
carefully	now	here	very
fast	again	outside	nearly
neatly	often	everywhere	greatly

An adverb can be placed in different parts of a sentence. It can come before the verb, after the verb, at the beginning of the sentence, or at the end of the sentence.

Before the Verb	We **often** play at the park.
After the Verb	We play **often** at the park.
At the Beginning of the Sentence	**Often,** we play at the park.
At the End of the Sentence	We play at the park **often.**

Try It!
Find five adverbs in the sentences below.
My baby sister is a sight at mealtime. Then she gets soggy crackers in her hair, mashed bananas here and there, and orange juice everywhere! She is happily learning to wear her food.

Prepositions and Prepositional Phrases

A **preposition** is a word that tells about the position or direction of a noun or pronoun.

Common Prepositions

about	above	across	after	against
along	around	at	before	behind
below	beside	between	by	down
for	from	in	inside	into
like	near	of	off	on
out	outside	over	through	to
under	underneath	up	with	without

A preposition always begins a group of words called a prepositional phrase. A **prepositional phrase** begins with a preposition and ends with a noun or pronoun. You will use prepositions in your writing to show where something is or where it is going.

The dog ran **down the road.**

Keisha is **across the street.**

Try It!

How many of the prepositions in the list above fit in the sentence below?

The rabbit jumped _____ the log.

Conjunctions and Interjections

A **conjunction** is a word that connects other words or groups of words. The most common conjunctions are *and, but,* and *or.*

It's raining *cats and dogs.*

Would you like *soup or salad?*

Marc *made and sold* his own cards.

Do you like *red or blue* better?

I play *soccer but not basketball.*

An **interjection** is a word or group of words that shows strong feelings. An interjection can stand alone with an exclamation point, or it can be part of a sentence. An interjection that shows very strong feeling is followed by an exclamation point. An interjection that shows mild feeling is connected to the sentence with a comma.

Stands Alone	Part of a Sentence
Oops! I almost fell on the ice!	**Hi,** it's good to see you!
Yes! I'd love to come to your party!	**Gee,** we'd better wear our raincoats.

Subjects and Predicates

Every sentence has a subject and a predicate. The **complete subject** is all the words that tell whom or what a sentence is about. The **simple subject** is the noun that tells who or what does or is something in the sentence.

> **The brown dog** lives in the city. (complete subject)
>
> The brown **dog** lives in the city. (simple subject)

A **compound subject** is two or more simple subjects connected by a conjunction.

> **Mary** and **Jack** live in the city.
>
> My **mother** and **father** are doctors.
>
> The **trees** and **buildings** are tall.

The **complete predicate** is all the words that tell what the subject is or does. The **simple predicate** is the verb that tells what the subject is or does.

> They **live in the city.** (complete predicate)
>
> They **live** in the city. (simple predicate)

A **compound predicate** is two or more predicates connected by a conjunction. A compound predicate tells two or more things about the subject.

> They **live** and **work** in the city.
>
> My parents **treat** and **cure** patients.

Simple and Compound Sentences

Simple Sentences

Sentences can be formed in different ways. A **simple sentence** has one subject and one predicate. The subject of a simple sentence can be simple or compound. So can the predicate.

Simple Subject Earth	**Simple Predicate** **is** the third planet from the sun.
Compound Subject Neptune and Pluto	**Simple Predicate** **are** the farthest planets from the sun.
Simple Subject The sun	**Compound Predicate** **shines** light and **sends** heat to earth.
Compound Subject Venus and Mars	**Compound Predicate** have been **photographed** and **mapped** by scientists.

Compound Sentences

A **compound sentence** is two or more simple sentences joined by a conjunction. A comma is placed before the conjunction in a compound sentence.

Simple Sentences
Jupiter is the biggest planet.   It has 16 moons.

Compound Sentence
Jupiter is the biggest planet, and it has 16 moons.

Sentence Problems

Sentence problems make writing hard to read and understand. This lesson describes three kinds of sentence problems and ways to correct them.

Fragments are incomplete sentences. A fragment can be missing a subject, a predicate, or both. Fix a fragment by adding what's missing.

Fragment: *Saturn many rings.*

Sentence: *Saturn* **has** *many rings.*

A **run-on sentence** is two or more sentences written together without a conjunction. Fix a run-on sentence by adding a comma and a conjunction or making two separate sentences.

Run-On Sentence	*Our sun is a star it looks big because we are close to it.*
Add a Conjunction	*Our sun is a star,* ***and*** *it looks big because we are close to it.*
Make Two Sentences	*Our sun is a star. It looks big because we are close to it.*

A **rambling sentence** is a sentence that goes on and on and has many conjunctions. Fix a rambling sentence by making separate sentences.

Rambling Sentence: *Neptune is the eighth planet from the sun and it has eight moons and its biggest moon is Triton.*

Corrected Sentences: *Neptune is the eighth planet from the sun. It has eight moons,* ***and*** *its biggest moon is Triton.*

Kinds of Sentences

Good writers use different kinds of sentences to make their writing interesting. There are four kinds of sentences.

Declarative sentences make statements or tell about facts. A declarative sentence ends with a period.

Soccer is my favorite sport.

Interrogative sentences ask questions. An interrogative sentence ends with a question mark.

What time does the game start?

Imperative sentences give commands or make requests. An imperative sentence ends with a period.

James, please go get the bag of soccer balls.

Exclamatory sentences show strong feelings. An exclamatory sentence ends with an exclamation point.

That was a great shot, Chloe!

Try It!

Four of the sentences below end with incorrect punctuation marks. Can you correct each one?

Who is going to be the goalie.

I love the feeling when I score a goal?

Amber, start the passing drill?

Shin guards protect your legs from kicks.

What's the score!

Usage

Usage is about how we use language when we speak and write. For example, the rules of usage tell you when to use *is* and when to use *are*. They tell you when to use *taller* and when to use *tallest*. Learning the rules of usage will help people better understand what you say and what you write.

Verb Tenses

Present, Past, and Future Tenses

The **tense** of a verb tells when an action happens. Verbs in the **present tense** tell what is happening now or what happens all the time.

> She **walks** to school.
>
> Josh **is** hungry.

Verbs in the **past tense** tell what has already happened. The past tense of an action verb is often formed by adding *-ed* to the base form of the verb.

> She **walked** to school.
>
> Josh **was** hungry.

Verbs in the **future tense** tell what will happen later. The future tense is often formed with the helping verb *will*.

> We **will go** to the library on Thursday.

Regular and Irregular Verbs

Verbs can be regular or irregular. A **regular verb** is one whose past tense is formed by adding -*ed* to the base verb. When a regular verb ends with *e*, the *e* is dropped before adding -*ed*.

Present Tense	talk	jump	smile	bake
Past Tense	talked	jumped	smiled	baked

An **irregular verb** is one whose past tense is not formed by following the rule for adding -*ed* to the base verb. The spelling of an irregular verb changes to form the past tense. Some irregular verbs are spelled differently when they are used with the helping verbs *has*, *have*, and *had*.

Common Irregular Verbs					
Present Tense	am	are	is	begin	come
	do	draw	eat	fall	give
	go	has	have	make	run
	say	see	seek	take	write
Past Tense	was	were	began	came	did
	drew	ate	fell	gave	went
	had	made	ran	said	saw
	sought	took	wrote		
Past Tense with *has*, *have*, or *had*	been	begun	come	done	drawn
	eaten	fallen	given	gone	had
	made	run	said	seen	sought
	taken	written			

Subject-Verb Agreement

   The subject of a sentence must agree with its verb. They both must be either singular or plural.

   When the subject is singular, or is a singular pronoun (*he, she,* or *it*), *-s* or *-es* is usually added to the base verb to form the present tense.

> learn + s = learns   Anna **learns** quickly.

   When a verb ends with *ch, sh, s, x,* or *z, -es* is added to form the present tense.

> wish + es = wishes   Bill **wishes** he could
>   visit Alaska.

   When a verb ends with a consonant and *y,* change the *y* to *i* and add *-es* to form the present tense.

> study + es = studies   Kim **studies** every night.

   When the subject is plural, or is a plural pronoun (*I, you, we,* or *they*), do not add *-s* or *-es* to the verb.

> work   The students **work** well together.

Irregular Verbs

Most past, present, and future tense **irregular verbs** are used with both singular and plural subjects. The singular and plural forms of these verbs are the same. The **irregular verbs** *be* and *have* change forms to make the present tense. They must always agree with their subjects.

Verb	Tense	Singular Subject	Plural Subject
be	present past	James **is** here. James **was** here.	The kids **are** here. The kids **were** here.
have	present past	Christina **has** lunch. Christina **had** lunch.	The girls **have** lunch. The girls **had** lunch.

Subject-Verb Agreement with Compound Subjects

Compound subjects must agree with their verbs. A compound subject has two or more simple subjects that have the same verb. The rules for subject-verb agreement are different for different conjunctions.

When *and* is the conjunction, *-s* is not added to the verb.

The girls **and** boys **play** soccer together.
Alex **and** Julie **play** on the same team.

When *or* is the conjunction, look at both subjects. If they are singular, *-s* is added to the verb. If the subjects are plural, *-s* is not added to the verb.

Cats **or** dogs **make** good pets. (plural subjects)
A cat **or** a dog **makes** a good pet. (singular subjects)

Forms of Adjectives and Adverbs

Some **adjectives** compare people, places, or things. A comparative adjective compares two people, places, or things.

Adjectives can compare one person, place, or thing with another. Add -*er* to most adjectives with one syllable. Use the word *more* before many adjectives with more than one syllable.

> The lion is **faster** than the zebra.
> Lions are **more graceful** than elephants.

Adjectives can compare three or more people, places, or things. Add -*est* to the end of most adjectives with one syllable. Use the word *most* before many adjectives with more than one syllable.

> The cheetah is the **fastest** animal on land.
> I think deer are the **most graceful** animals of all.

Some adjectives that compare have special forms.

> Sue is a **better** singer than Rachel.
> Grace is the **best** singer in the class.

Adverbs can compare actions. Add -*er* and -*est* to most short adverbs. Use *more* and *most* with adverbs ending in -*ly*.

> Jan left **earlier** than Lee.
> Kim left **earliest** of all.
> Ben talked **more quietly** than Josh.
> Ben talked **most quietly** of all.

Contractions

A **contraction** is a word made by joining two words and taking out one or more letters. An apostrophe shows where the letters are missing.

I am = I'm	they are = they're
you are = you're	I will = I'll
she is = she's	you will = you'll
it is = it's	he will = he'll
we are = we're	it will = it'll

Negative words are the word *no* and all words that mean *no*. Many contractions are negative words because they are made from the word *not*.

are not = aren't	had not = hadn't
will not = won't	cannot = can't
has not = hasn't	would not = wouldn't
is not = isn't	did not = didn't
do not = don't	should not = shouldn't
was not = wasn't	does not = doesn't

A **double negative** occurs when *two* negative words are used to express a single idea instead of *one* negative word. Many contractions use the negative word *not*. As a result, double negatives sometimes find their way into our speech and writing. Watch for the contraction trap, however, to avoid double negatives.

Incorrect: He does**n't** know **nothing** about karate.
  Correct: He doesn't know anything about karate.
  Correct: He knows nothing about karate.

Incorrect: We do**n't** have **no** lesson today.
  Correct: We don't have a lesson today.
  Correct: We have no lesson today.

Mechanics

The rules of mechanics are very important in writing. How and when to use punctuation marks is part of mechanics. Knowing when to use capital letters is a part of mechanics. Writers who know and follow these rules make it much easier for readers to understand what they write.

End Punctuation

Periods are used as end punctuation in sentences. Periods are also used in other ways.

▶ Periods end sentences that make statements.

February is the shortest month of the year.

▶ Periods end sentences that make demands or requests.

Please come to my party on Saturday.

▶ Periods are used after the initials in a person's name.

E. B. White wrote *Charlotte's Web* and *Stuart Little*.

▶ Periods are used after some abbreviations.

Jan. (January)   Mon. (Monday)

▶ Periods are used after abbreviations of people's titles.

Ms.   Mrs.   Mr.   Dr.   Jr.

▶ Periods are not used in some abbreviations where each letter stands for a word.

VCR (videocassette recorder)

Question marks are used to end sentences that ask questions.

Where is the library?
Do you have any brothers or sisters?

Exclamation points are used to end sentences that show strong feelings. Exclamation points are also used after interjections.

Wow! Please come back soon!

Commas

Commas are punctuation marks. They are used to separate words or set them off from the rest of the sentence.

▶ Commas are used between the name of a day and the year in a date.

Neil Armstrong walked on the moon on July 20, 1969.

▶ Commas are used between the names of a city and state or country.

Columbus, Ohio
Tokyo, Japan

▶ Commas are used after the greeting and the closing of a friendly letter.

Greetings: Dear Grandpa,   Dear Mary,
Closings: Your friend,   Truly,   With love,

▶ A comma is used between series of words or phrases.

We saw bison, moose, bears, and eagles in the park.

▶ A comma is used to set off the words of a speaker from other words in the sentence.

Dad said, " You earn money by raking the leaves."

▶ A comma is used after a person's name, after the words *yes* and *no*, and after a mild interjection at the beginning of a sentence.

Mom, can I have a pet snake?
Yes, when you have a house of your own.
Oh, that's a long time to wait.

▶ A comma is used before the conjunction in a compound sentence.

We sat on the porch swing, **and** we watched the sunset.

Quotation Marks and Underlining

Quotation marks set off the exact words of a speaker or another writer. When you write, put quotation marks before and after the exact words of a speaker or writer. Use a comma to separate the exact words from the rest of the sentence. Place end punctuation for the exact words inside the quotation marks.

Mom said patiently, "I'll wait right here for you."

"Go, Zoe!" Dad yelled, "Score a goal!"

Quotation marks set off the titles of short stories, poems, songs, and the chapters of books.

We always sing "Home on the Range" because our music teacher is from Wyoming.

I love the poems "Double-Tail Dog" and "Smart."

When you are writing, use **underlining** to set off the titles of books, magazines, newspapers, television shows, movies, and plays. Put these titles in italics if you are using a computer.

Our teacher is reading *The Wind in the Willows* to our class.

Mom bought the movie *Tarzan* because she liked it so much.

The *National Geographic World* magazine for kids has great photos.

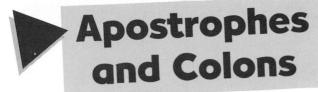

Apostrophes and Colons

An **apostrophe** is a punctuation mark used to make possessive nouns and contractions. Here are ways to use apostrophes to make possessive nouns.

▶ Add an apostrophe and *-s* to singular nouns.

Mom**'s** pancakes are the best.

▶ Add an apostrophe and *-s* to plural nouns that do not end in *s*.

We put our drawings in the Children's Art Show.

▶ Add only an apostrophe to plural nouns that end in *-s*.

The students**'** gifts were collected.

▶ Add an apostrophe to show where letters have been left out in a contraction.

cannot = can't   I am = I'm   we will = we'll

A **colon** is a punctuation mark used to write hours and minutes. A colon is also used before a list in a sentence and after the greeting in a business letter.

▶ Use a colon between the hour and minute numbers.

We usually eat dinner at **6:30.**

▶ Use a colon before a list of things in a sentence.

I always get the same fruits at the store: apples, bananas, oranges, grapes, and pears.

▶ Use a colon after the greeting in a business letter.

Dear Store Owner: Dear Editor: Dear Mr. Clark:

Hyphens and Parentheses

A **hyphen** divides a word with two or more syllables at the end of a line. The hyphen shows that the word continues on the next line.

> Aunt Lynda grows plants in her green-
> house.

A word can be divided with a hyphen only when at least three letters will be on each line.

Incorrect	Robert placed the pots a- bove the refrigerator.
Correct	Robert placed the pots above the refrig- erator.

Parentheses set off words that add extra information to a sentence. Parentheses are put at the beginning and end of the words.

> Dogs and cats are both mammals (see page 744).
>
> Dogs and cats are both mammals (warm-blooded vertebrates).

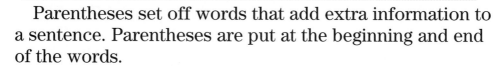

Try It!

A hyphen and parentheses are missing from the sentence below. Can you find where they go?

When I was little which wasn't really that long ago I liked to eat pickle sand wiches.

Capitalization

Beginning Words

Capitalize the first word of a sentence.

My dog always seems happy to see me.

Capitalize the first word of a quotation even if it's not the beginning of the sentence.

He laughed and said, "**T**hat joke gets funnier every time I hear it."

Names

Capitalize the names of people and pets.

Laura likes our little dog, **P**eanut.

Capitalize the pronoun *I*.

The teacher said **I** could help serve the apples.

Capitalize words used as names.

Dad and **G**randpa took us fishing at the lake.

Titles

Capitalize people's titles and initials.

Dr. Diana **A.** Taylor   **M**rs. **R. J.** Sanchez

Capitalize the first word, last word, and all important words in titles of books, magazines, and newspapers.

Little House in the Big Woods is my favorite book.

Capitalize the titles of movies, plays, and TV shows.

I saw the movie *A Bug's Life* five times.

Languages

Capitalize the names of languages.

Maria can speak both **E**nglish and **S**panish.

Place Names and Geographic Names

Capitalize the names of countries, cities, states, oceans, rivers, mountains, and lakes.

> United States of America
> Boston   Oregon   Pacific Ocean
> Mississippi River   Lake Erie   Rocky Mountains

Special Dates, Holidays, Historical Periods, and Special Events

Capitalize the names of months, days, and holidays.

> November   Friday   Thanksgiving

Capitalize the names of historical periods and special events.

> The Computer Age   The Civil War   The Olympics

Parts of Letters

Capitalize the first word in the greeting and closing of a letter.

> Dear Madeline,   Yours truly,

Abbreviations and Acronyms

Capitalize abbreviations of proper nouns.

Wed. (Wednesday)

NBA (National Basketball Association)

Capitalize acronyms.

AMSLAN = American Sign Language

HOPE = Health Opportunity for People Everywhere

Try It!

Find the three capitalization mistakes in the sentence below.

Every january, my family watches the super bowl.

Writing Connection

When you're writing, be sure to capitalize the first word of every sentence. Also capitalize the first word of a quotation, proper nouns and people's titles and initials. Capitalize the first word and all important words in the titles of books, magazines, and newspapers. The titles of movies, plays and television shows, as well as the names of languages, need to be capitalized also. Finally, capitalize place names and geographic names; special dates, holidays, historical periods, and special events; parts of letters; and abbreviations and acronyms.

Glossary

A

abbreviation   the shortening of a word, such as St. for Street. Most abbreviations are followed by a period.

across-the-curriculum words   words that explain terms for math, science, social studies, health, or other topics

action verbs   verbs that show the actions of someone or something in a sentence

adjective   a word that describes a noun or a pronoun

adverb   a word that describes a verb, adjective, or another adverb. An adverb tells how, when, where, or how much something happens.

alliteration   using several words together that have the same beginning consonant sound

antonym   a word that means the opposite, or almost the opposite, of another word

articles   *a* and *an* (indefinite) and *the* (definite)

audience   the person or people who read what you write

awkward sentence   a confusing or unclear sentence

B

body (letter)   the main part of a letter. It includes the specific information you want the reader to know.

body (news story)   the part of a news story that comes after the lead paragraph in which more details and information are given

body (paragraph)   usually the middle part of a paragraph that gives supporting details for the topic sentence

book review   a piece of writing in which you tell others what you thought about a book, either fiction or nonfiction

business letter   a formal letter written to an organization or company for one special reason: to express a complaint, to express a concern, or to request information

byline   tells who wrote a news story

C

caption   a sentence or phrase written under a picture or illustration that tells more about the picture or explains it

chain of events   a type of graphic organizer that shows events in the order in which they happen

common nouns   nouns that name any person, place, thing, or idea and start with a lowercase letter

compound predicate   shows two or more things about the subject

compound sentence   two or more simple sentences joined together by a conjunction

compound subject   two or more simple subjects connected by a conjunction

conjunction   a word that connects other words or ideas. The words *and, but,* and *or* are conjunctions.

context clues   word or sentence clues from the text that help you figure out the meaning of unknown words

conventions   the rules one follows when writing. These include spelling, grammar, punctuation, capitalization, and usage.

D

declarative sentence   a sentence that makes a statement and ends with a period

definite article   the article *the* that identifies specific people, places, things, or ideas

description   gives details about a person, place, thing, or action

details   statements, facts, and opinions that support the main idea of a paragraph or story

dialogue   the talk or conversation between two or more characters in a story or play

drafting   the part of the writing process in which you write a draft, or first try, of what you want to say

E

editing/proofreading   the part of the writing process where you read your writing to check for mistakes in grammar, spelling, punctuation, and capitalization

effective beginning   a beginning of a story that grabs the reader's attention and makes them want to read more

effective ending   an ending of a story that brings the piece of writing to a close and keeps the reader thinking about it

end rhyme   using rhyming words at the end of lines of poetry

exclamatory sentence   a sentence that shows strong feeling and ends with an exclamation point

expository paragraph   a paragraph that gives or explains information

expository writing   a type of writing based on facts, such as giving a summary, giving directions to a location, explaining a process, or writing a report

F

fantasy   a story that has characters, places, or events that could not exist in the real world

fragment   an incomplete sentence. It can be missing a subject, predicate, or both.

free-verse poem   poem that does not rhyme or have a pattern

future-tense verb   a verb that shows what will happen later

H

helping verb   the first part of a verb phrase, such as *was, were, had,* or *has*

homophone   words that sound the same but have different spellings and meanings

I

imperative sentence   a sentence that gives a command or makes a request and ends with a period or exclamation point

indefinite article   the articles *a* and *an* that refer to a general group of people, places, things, or ideas

interjection   a word that shows strong feelings. It can sometimes stand alone as a sentence.

interrogative sentence   a type of sentence that asks a question and ends with a question mark

irregular plural nouns   nouns that do not follow the rule for most plural nouns, such as *child* and *children*

irregular verb   a verb that does not follow the rule for adding *-ed* to form the past tense

L

lead   the first paragraph of a news story that answers the five Ws

learning log   a type of journal or notebook in which you keep a record of what you learned about something

linking verb   a state-of-being verb that links the subject of the sentence with a word in the predicate

M

main verb   the last word in a verb phrase, usually an action verb

metaphor   compares two unlike things without using the words *like* or *as*

mood   the feeling the reader or listener gets when reading or hearing a piece of writing

mystery   a piece of writing in which something happens and it is not clear how or why it happened

N

narrative paragraph   a paragraph that tells a story

nonrhyming poetry   poetry in which the words at the ends of the lines do not rhyme

nouns   words that name everything. For example, people, places, things, and ideas are nouns.

O

observation   what one sees and hears during the happening of an event

onomatopoeia   a word that imitates the sound it describes, such as *swish* and *pop*

order words   words that tell in what order things happen, such as *first, next,* and *last*

P

paragraph   a group of sentences about one idea

past-tense verb   a verb that shows what has already happened

pattern poetry   poetry in which the lines follow patterns for length and number of syllables

personal narrative   a form of writing in which the writer tells something that has really happened in his or her own life

personification   describes animals or things as if they were people

persuasive paragraph   a paragraph that gives the writer's opinion on a topic and reasons or examples to support it

persuasive writing   a type of writing in which the writer tries to persuade the reader to think, feel, or act in a certain way

plural nouns nouns that name more than one person

plural possessive nouns plural nouns that show who owns something

plural pronoun a pronoun that takes the place of a noun that names more than one person or thing

poetry a type of writing in which the sound and meaning of words are combined to create images and feelings

point of view the thoughts of the person telling the story

possessive nouns nouns that show who owns something

possessive pronoun a pronoun that shows who owns something

predicate tells what the subject is or does in a sentence

prefix a word part added to the beginning of a base word, changing the meaning

preposition a word that shows position or direction

prepositional phrase a phrase that begins with a preposition and ends with a noun or pronoun

present tense verb a verb that shows what is happening now or what happens all the time

prewriting the part of the writing process where you choose a topic, gather ideas, and make a plan

pronouns words that take the place of nouns

proofreading marks the special marks one uses when proofreading a piece of writing

proper nouns nouns that name a specific person, place, thing, or idea and always start with a capital letter

publishing the part of the writing process where you share your writing

purpose your reason for writing. The purpose could be to persuade, entertain, or inform.

R

realistic story   a made-up story with characters who seem real and a plot with events that could really happen

regular verb   a verb that forms the past tense by adding *-ed* to the past tense verb

research report   a report that gives information about facts, ideas, or events using sources such as the Internet, books, magazines, or newspapers

revising   a part of the writing process in which you make changes to improve what you have written

rhyming poetry   poetry that uses rhyming words at the ends of the lines

rhythm   a pattern of sounds in prose or poetry created by repetition of words, phrases, or sounds

S

sentence fluency   the way you arrange your sentences in a piece of writing so that they read smoothly

simile   compares two unlike things using the words *like* or *as*. Example: She is as cute as a button.

simple predicate   the verb that tells what the subject is or does in a sentence

simple sentence   has one subject and one predicate

simple subject   the noun that tells who or what does or is something in a sentence

singular possessive nouns   singular nouns that show who owns something

singular pronoun   a pronoun that takes the place of a noun that names one person or thing

spatial order   a type of graphic organizer that shows details in a chosen order, such as left-to-right or top-to-bottom

state-of-being verb   a verb that does not show action but shows a condition or state of being, such as *am, are, was, were*

story map   a type of graphic organizer used to plan a story, including characters, setting, and plot

subject   who or what a sentence is about

subject-verb agreement   when the verb agrees with the subject of the sentence. They both must be singular or plural.

suffix   a word part added to the end of a base word, changing the meaning

summary   writing that tells the main idea and main points of a longer piece of writing

superlative form   the form of an adjective or adverb that compares more than two people, places, or things

supporting sentence   tells more about the idea in the topic sentence

synonym   a word that means the same, or almost the same, meaning as another word

T

tall tale   a made-up story that usually exaggerates or stretches the truth

tense   the form of a verb that tells when an action happens, such as in the present, past, or future

topic sentence   a sentence that tells the main idea of a paragraph. Topic sentences occur most often in expository or persuasive writing.

top-to-bottom graphic organizer   a type of graphic organizer that organizes the details from a top-to-bottom approach, used when writing a description

triplet   poetry that has three lines of rhyming words

U

underlining   a punctuation mark used to set off the titles of books, magazines, newspapers, TV shows, movies, or plays

V

variety   using different words and sentence types to make a piece of writing more interesting

Venn diagram   a type of graphic organizer used to compare or contrast two things

verb phrase   one or more helping verbs followed by the main verb

verbs   words that show action or state-of-being

voice   the tone or sound of your writing. The voice of a piece of writing changes as the audience changes.

W

web   a type of graphic organizer that has the main idea inside a circle in the middle with lines connecting to bubbles that contain supporting details

writing process   a plan to follow when writing. The steps are prewriting, drafting, revising, editing/proofreading, and publishing.

Index

The index is a list of words and page numbers. It lists the different things that are in the Handbook. The words are in alphabetical order. You look in the list for the word you want to find. Then you look at the page number of the Handbook where it can be found. The index is a good tool. Learn to use it. It can save you a lot of time.

S

T

U

V

W

▶ Photo Credits: